JASON LEE
Winner of the Northwest

The four Indians swam rivers, hid from hostile Indians, hunted for food, sometimes lived on only berries and fruit. "My moccasins are worn out," said one, and no wonder. They had traveled nearly 3000 miles on foot. For what? To seek the Book of Heaven from the white man.

The story captured the imaginations and hearts of Christendom. Methodists responded by sending Jason Lee to Oregon. Lee loved the Northwest when he read about it, and he loved it even more when he reached the end of the Oregon Trail and saw its rivers and forests and fertile soil and its Indians and rugged pioneer whites.

Jason built his mission on the banks of the Willamette, then he lobbied his Mission Board to send more personnel so he could open branch mission houses. He spoke in churches urging people to move to the land of the setting sun and help to build a Christian Oregon. And he lobbied Congress to establish Oregon as a Territory.

Tragedy stalked Jason, and he died in the noon of life, so he had no opportunity to enjoy triumph. But in after years, when the state needed to select two of its native sons to honor in the Statuary Hall of the Capitol Building in Washington, D.C., it was obvious to its citizens that one of them should be Jason Lee.

Today his statue stands not only in the National Hall, but also on the lawn of Oregonians' own Capitol Building in Salem. And nearby is a statue of a Methodist circuit rider, reminding viewers of the part the Book of Heaven played in the history of the Northwest.

ABOUT THE AUTHOR

Prize-winning author, Dr. Charles Ludwig, grew up in Kenya, the son of missionaries. He has traveled in scores of countries and preached in many of them. He has written 1500 articles, stories, and serials, as well as fifty books. His writings have appeared in Braille and in fourteen languages, and have been published on six continents. A number of his books have been read or dramatized on world-wide radio.

In gathering material for this book, the author and his wife, Mary, started at the beginning of the Oregon Trail in Missouri and followed the trail, visiting many places along the way. In addition, they made two other trips to the Northwest. He says that he thoroughly enjoyed researching the geographical and historical backgrounds for this story of Jason Lee.

ABOUT THE ARTIST

Peggy Trabalka lives in historic Milford, Michigan. There she does what she loves most—turning stories into beautiful picutres. She is a member of galleries and artistic clubs and illustrates children's books. Peggy has a passion for art! She feels an illustration should be a personal experience. She comes from a long line of storytellers; she enjoys making history come alive.

An artist almost since birth, Peggy attended Cass Technical School to polish her skills. She makes her living as a free-lance commercial artist.

Jason Lee

Winner of the Northwest

by

Charles Ludwig

Illustrated by

Peggy Trabalka

Dedicated to those readers who have the courage — and will power — to ignore the pressures of the herd in order that their lives might count.

COPYRIGHT © 1992 by Mott Media, Inc.

Kurt Dietsch, Cover Artist

LIBRARY OF CONGRESS CATALOGING IN PUBLICATION DATA

Ludwig, Charles, 1918.
    Jason Lee: Winner of the Northwest / by Charles Ludwig, Illustrated by Peggy Trabalka.

    p.   cm.—(Sowers Series)
    Bibliography: p.165
    Includes index.

    SUMMARY: A biography of the missionary to the Indians who helped to open up Oregon to settlers.
    ISBN 0-88062-161-3
    1. Lee, Jason, 1803-1845—Juvenile literature. 2. Pioneers—Oregon—Biography—Juvenile literature. 3. Missionaries—Oregon—Biography—Juvenile literature. 4. Oregon—History—To 1859—Juvenile literature. 5. Methodist Church—Oregon—Missions—Juvenile literature. 6. Indians of North America—Oregon—Missions—Juvenile literature. [1.Lee, Jason, 1803-1845. 2. Missionaries. 3. Pioneers.] I. Trabalka, Peggy, ill. II. Title. III. Series.
F880.L494L83 1991
979.5ₑ03ₑ092—dc20
[B]
[92]   ·   90-6329
                                               CIP
                                               AC

ISBN 0-88062-161-3   Paperbound

CONTENTS

ACKNOWLEDGMENTS

I owe special thanks to the librarians at Willamett University, and especially to Mary Dorsett from the United Methodist Commission on Archives and History. She spent an entire afternoon with my wife and me while she pointed out important historical spots connected with Jason Lee, both in and just outside Salem. Mary Dorsett also lent us a copy of the valuable book in which was recorded the speeches and the program that followed when Jason Lee's remains were reburied in Salem. Thanks are also due to my efficient editor, Dr. Ruth Beechick.

1
Prisoner of Fate

Fourteen-year-old Jason Lee lifted the ax high above his head, then with a mighty swing, buried the blade in the log. Smiling with satisfaction, he realized that, although he was the youngest in his family, he could cut and stack an entire cord of sugar-maple in less than two hours. This was a record no one in Stanstead could break. Moreover, he had already been placed in charge of a crew of adult men. Even so, he was utterly miserable.

Later, while warming his hands at the fireplace, he grumbled to his brother, "I'm a prisoner of fate."

"Nonsense!" exploded Elias, his senior by twenty-five years, and oldest of the fifteen children in the family. "You're six feet tall and are still growin'. Pretty soon people will bend their necks and inquire, 'What's the altitude up there?'"

"And when they do," replied Jason as he twisted the lobe of his right ear, "I'll say, it's rainin'. Then I'll spit."

"You mean you'll spit on them?" Elias smiled as he poked the fire.

"Nope. You know better than that! I wouldn't hurt a flea. That is I wouldn't hurt a *good* flea. I'll just spit on the ground." He demonstrated by spitting into the fire.

As the glowing coals sizzled, Elias' face became thoughtful. "Why do you think you're a prisoner of fate?" He slanted his eyes toward his baby brother.

"Because of many things."

"For example?"

"In the first place I don't know whether I'm a Canadian or an American."

"The answer to that is easy. You are an American."

"But Stanstead is in Lower Canada, and I was born and raised there; three miles north of Stanstead!"

"True, but both our parents and all our grandparents were born in New England. That means we are as American as the Liberty Bell. The fact that you were born in Canada means nothing. If a cat climbs into an oven and has kittens in the oven they're still kittens and not biscuits. But there would be nothing wrong in being a Canadian. Some of the finest people in the world are Canadians."

After they both laughed, Elias added, "And please remember that our father fought in the battle of Lexington!"

"All that's wonderful," replied Jason nodding his head, "and I'm very proud of my parents. But, Elias, I sometimes feel that I'm like the crack in the Liberty Bell."

"You're like the crack?" Elias's eyes widened.

"Yes, I'm like the crack. I keep it from being rung."

"How could that be?"

"Pa died when I was three, and I have no memory of him." Jason felt a lump forming in his throat. "He told *you* about the war; and he told *you* about his famous relatives; and he played with *you*. I don't even remember ever sitting on his lap. But the worst part of my problem is that because I'm an orphan I haven't been able to get an education. Every day while I'm chopping wood or digging ditches I hear children as they go to school.

"I want to amount to something. But now—" He threw out his hands in a gesture of despair. "Now I have to work instead of going to school. I'll never amount to anything. I'll just be a woodchopper all my life."

"It's about time you two stopped talking and came to the table," announced their sister Mary, who kept house for them.

After Elias said the blessing, they each helped themselves to mashed potatoes, covered them with brown gravy, and cut a generous slice of buffalo steak. Between bites Elias commented, "Jason, I remember the June day in 1803 when you were born. Exciting events were happening at that time."

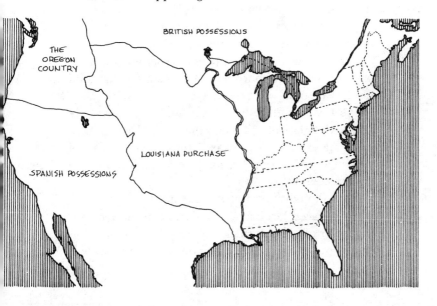

"They were?" asked Jason.

"Yes, that very year President Jefferson bought the Louisiana Territory from France, and everyone didn't agree with Jefferson. Massachusetts and New York even threatened to secede, for they said he had violated the Constitution by not having the consent of the Senate. Even so, with the flick of a pen, Jefferson doubled the size of the United States—and we're still growin'! Jason, you chose to be born at just the right time!"

"Pa was sure glad to see you," added Mary, "even though he already had eight boys and six girls. You were boy number nine! Both of our parents really loved you. And they hugged you so much the rest of us were plumb jealous."

Elias cut another portion of buffalo. "This buffalo almost got away from me," he chuckled. "My first shot barely nicked his behind. But my horse helped me keep up with him and I blew a hole in his heart. He's a little special and so I'm going to have my share." Elias laughed. Then he turned to Jason. "You think that because you're an orphan Pa didn't have any influence over you. That's a mistake. You're almost a spittin' image of him. You have the same blue eyes, the same thick jaws, the same light hair, and the same stubbornness that possessed him. Pa never gave up!"

Jason's eyes glistened at this, and he accidentally knocked a glass of milk onto the floor. "And you're just as awkward as he was," put in Mary, as she rushed to get a mop. "Pa had a way of bumping into almost everything."

Elias thoughtfully finished his portion of buffalo. Then he faced Jason again. This time he glowed with the ferver of a circuit rider at a revival meeting. "You think you're behind because you can't go to school,

but that isn't so. You've read more books than most
teachers. And both Ma and Pa believed that God has
His hand on you. I agree with them. Jason Lee, God
has a special, a very special, work for you too.''

Jason froze. "I'm not interested in working for
God!" he stormed angrily. "I want to live my own
life in my own way." He doubled his fists and glared.

Elias smiled. "I know exactly how you feel, for I
once felt that way myself. But God has a way of
slipping hooks into the jaws of those He especially
needs; and when He does, those who are hooked
usually try to get away. They pull and tug just like
a trout. Some of 'em get away by breakin' the line.
But when they do, the line usually gets snarled on a
root or somethin' and they just die havin'
accomplished nothin'. As for me, I want to make my
life count." He concluded with a firm smile.

His face flushed, Jason stood up. "I'd better go to
my room," he snapped. "I'm reading about the
Northwest. That's the land of the future."

"The Northwest!" exclaimed Elias.

"Yes, the Northwest. That's a marvelous country;
and someday it'll belong to the United States." Jason
sat down again.

"The Northwest is no place for you," said Elias.
"A friend of mine told me that the whole place is
crammed with scalp-hunting Indians; and, besides,
no one wants it."

"Oh, but in time, when the truth is discovered,
everyone will want it—especially Britain and the
United States. It won't be long before both sides will
claim it. Even so, it will become part of the United
States, and that's the smack-dab truth!"

"What makes you say that?" asked Elias as he
rocked back in his chair.

"Because Robert Gray, who discovered the

Columbia River, was an American,'' Jason began.
He wanted to tell a lot more from his reading, but
Elias interrupted him.

"Time's gettin' away," Elias said, "I must lead
family worship.''

"Go ahead,'' grumbled Jason sarcastically. "I'm
as ready as I'll ever be.''

"Our lesson is from Paul's first letter to the
Corinthians,'' said Elias. He spoke calmly, even
though Jason indicated his contempt by sullenly
glaring at his plate. "We'll start with the 18th verse
of the 12th chapter of First Corinthians.''

Articulating carefully, he read:

> But now hath God set the members every one of them in the
> body, as it hath pleased him. And if they were all one member,
> where were the body? But now are they many members, yet
> but one body. And the eye cannot say unto the hand, I have
> no need of thee: nor again the head to the feet, I have no need
> of you . . . .

"All of that means that each of us is a part of the
body of Christ,'' explained Elias, "and we're all
equally important. Now let us kneel and pray.''

After Mary and Elias prayed, they waited for
Jason's customary prayer. But this time Jason remained silent. After a long wait, Mary and Elias stood up
and Jason headed for the stairs.

Jason reached the third step on the way to his room
when Mary handed him a new candle. "The
Northwest *is* an interesting place,'' she said.

"Have you read about it?''

"No, but friends have told me about it.''

"What did they say?''

"One story is that there is a place called the Burnt
Cliffs that is full of devils about eighteen inches high.''

"Do you believe that?'' Jason frowned.

"I-I don't know." She shrugged. "But it is sort of scary." She hesitated. "Tell me about Robert Gray."

"I'm going to read more about him tonight. I'll tell you what I've learned in the morning."

Jason lit the new candle, slipped beneath the bearskin, and eagerly reached for the pamphlet that sketched the life of Robert Gray, and his discovery of the Columbia.

The story was so interesting he kept flipping the pages, totally unconscious of time. Finally his candle burned out, and a short time later the grandfather clock bonged twice, indicating that it was 2 a.m. Reluctantly, Jason closed his eyes and was soon asleep.

The next morning while wolfing his breakfast of ham and eggs, Jason hogged the table talk by relating what he'd learned about Captain Robert Gray. "You see Columbus thought that America was merely a part of Asia. His successors knew better. But even they thought America was simply a string of large islands. And because of that, they tried to find a 'northwest passage' which, they believed, would make a short route between the islands to China.

"While searching, they discovered that the northwest coast was full of beaver, and that they could buy pelts from the Indians for just a few trinkets; and then sell them in China for a hundred times more than they paid."

"You're not eating your ham and eggs," cautioned Mary.

"All right. All right," replied Jason holding up his hand. "But this is interesting. The Indians with whom they traded soon discovered that they could get higher prices for their pelts. The traders then decided the best way to buy cheap furs was to find Indians in new areas of the country who did not know the real value of their furs. So they tried to find a way to the interior where they would be unknown to the Indians.

"When they asked about a route the Indians told them of a great river which they called Ouragan."

"Is that where we get the name Oregon?" asked Mary.

"It is. But due to the sandbars across its mouth, it was very hard to find. While searching for a northwest passage, Sir Francis Drake touched the coast of Oregon in 1579, but he didn't even see the river. Two hundred years later Captain James Cook also visited Oregon in search of a northwest passage. But like the others, he missed the great river.

"Like huge gates, the sandbars kept the secret."

Following a nervous glance at the clock, Elias said, "You'd better hurry up. I have to go to work."

"I'm nearing the best part," replied Jason.

"A few years later, Captain Robert Gray was curious about that mysterious river the Indians called the Ouragan. He was already famous for sailing around the world and he returned to the Northwest in 1792. While hugging the coast, he sailed south from what is now known as Gray's Harbor. Just beyond Deception Bay, he continued east past Cape Disappointment into the Ouragan." Jason managed a bite of breakfast now and then during his story.

"And how did he get past the sandbars?" asked Mary.

"He crossed over them because it was high tide."

"And why did they call it Cape Disappointment?"

"It was given that name by Captain John Meares in 1788. The breakers and sandbars had kept him from discovering the river; and it's good that they did, for he was a British naval officer sailing under Portuguese papers. Had he discovered the river, there would have been no end of argument as to which nation had the rights of discovery, Britain or Portugal,'' Jason laughed.

''Since Gray discovered the river, he had the right to name it; and so he named it Columbia's, as if it belonged to his ship the Columbia.''

Mary asked, ''Does Gray's discovery mean that all of Oregon belongs to the United States?''

''Certainly not! There are complications. One snag that all but ruins our claim involves an Englishman, Captain George Vancouver. Another concerns the wastepaper basket of Robert Gray's niece.'' He glanced at the clock and grasped the door handle. I'll tell you more later. I've hired a new man and I'd better get to the job early so I can tell him what to do.''

2
Lure of the Northwest

With an ax over his shoulder, Jason waited for his men to appear. While he waited, he stepped over to the old log house where he was born. He walked around it and his mind filled with nostalgia. The old brick chimney was still standing, and the not-quite-square windows were just as they had been. He tried to remember what it used to be like inside, but all he could remember was the massive stone fireplace together with the giant black tomcat who liked to warm himself by the fire and scrub his whiskers with an oversized paw.

Memories of Tom were vivid. He especially remembered the way the white-pawed gentleman comforted him by rubbing against his legs and purring each time after he'd been spanked. On those occasions as Tom's body rumbled, Jason was convinced that his old hunter friend would remain loyal until death.

Wading through the weeds that surrounded the sagging house, Jason looked north. There his gaze rested on a hill covered with dense forests of trees.

From that elevation he knew that he could view the rolling plains to the south. Walled in by purple mountains, the magnificent panorama covered a three-hundred mile circumference.

Jeff London, the new man, then showed up. He was a square-shouldered, solidly-built individual who hid much of his face behind a red beard and thick moustache. During his investigation, Jason had learned that Jeff was a fearless, adventure-loving person. In the War of 1812, he fought with the British and was present at the burning of the White House. Later, he went as far west as St. Louis, and helped various mountain men get their loads assembled for trips to the Northwest.

After Jason introduced Jeff to his duties, he asked a question. "What do you know about the Northwest?"

"You mean Oregon?"

"Yes, Oregon."

"Wal, I used to see a lot of mountain men when they returned to civilization. Some of 'em had nearly been scalped; one or two had fought grizzly bears."

"What are grizzly bears like?" asked Jason. His eyes widened as he awaited an answer.

"They're tough. Some weigh as much as a thousand pounds, and their claws are sometimes six inches long. But they can't climb trees."

"Why?"

"Because their claws are too blunt."

Noticing other workers coming, Jeff said, "Most of your men are Yankees. Will they hate me because my father was a Tory and I fought with the British?"

"Of course not. People here at Stanstead get along even though some are American and others are Canadian. We're so close to Vermont, the boundary line runs right through one of the houses. Kitchen's in the United States. Parlor's in Canada.'' He laughed.

After a pause Jason asked, ''Would you like to be a mountain man?''

''In some ways yes and in some ways no.''

Their conversation was interrupted by the arrival of the rest of the crew.

''Well, I guess we'd better get to work,'' said Jason.

As the men swung their axes and piled maple firewood into cords, Jason's mind kept returning to Jeff and what he said about the life of mountain men. During a break for lunch, he approached Jeff. ''How hard would it be to become a mountain man?''

''Not very. All you'd have to do is to go to Saint Louis and join up with someone. But if I were you I wouldn't even think about it. Most of 'em die or get killed. You should see some I've seen when they come back all chewed by grizzlies. Oregon's interestin'. Big mountains. Lots of fish. Deserts. Blue skies. Waterfalls. Lakes. But it ain't no place for a gentleman.''

''Would you know where I could get a book about Lewis and Clark's expedition to the Northwest?''

''Sure do. I have an uncle who was a schoolteacher and he has a whole shelf of books about both them and Oregon.''

Jason's eyes glistened. ''W-would I be able to borrow some?''

''Of course. But you'd have to be real careful because my uncle's awful particular about his books.''

A week later, with the book about the Lewis and Clark expedition in hand, Jason was so eager to start reading he was tempted to dismiss the men early. That evening after he swallowed his supper, he asked Mary to give him some extra candles. Then he scooted up the steps two at a time.

Pillow doubled high, and two candles glowing, Jason opened the book. He felt like Aladdin with the magic lamp. After the first paragraph, he discovered that the journals of this pair were alive with interest. The explorers described the characteristics of the land, recorded observations about the Indians, related how they killed strange birds, and how they stuffed their skins so that artists and scientists back home could study them. Jason kept reading until his candles flickered out. Then he tried to sleep. But sleep would not come. Thoughts about bears, wild Indians, rivers, and snowcapped mountains kept splashing into his brain. Finally, he dozed off. But now he was tormented by realistic dreams. In the final and most terrifying one, a huge grizzly came after him. The brute had just opened its mouth to crush his skull when he awakened.

While shuddering at the window, he was horrified to notice that the sun was already above the horizon. He had overslept! This meant he'd have to hurry.

After Elias read from the Bible and prayed, he commented that Mississippi is no longer a territory. "It has just been admitted to the Union as the twentieth state. When the Louisiana Purchase is divided into additional states we'll really be on our way to becoming one of the greatest nations on earth." He shook his head. "That'll be somethin' to crow about. Yes, that'll be somethin' to crow about!"

"The Louisiana Purchase *was* a great bargain," agreed Jason, "and we got all of it for only about four cents an acre. But just wait until the Northwest becomes a part of the Union, and someday it will!" He toyed with his right ear.

"Last night I learned something interesting," he said.

"What did you learn?" asked Elias.

"I learned that in 1803—about six months *before* I was born—President Jefferson asked Congress to consider sending some trailblazers to the Northwest to see what was out there; Congress agreed, and in 1804, a year *after* I was born, Lewis and Clark started out on their long journey."

"Well, now you know that you were born during exciting times," replied Elias with a laugh as he refilled his cup with coffee. "That should make you feel good."

"Before we start talking about Lewis and Clark," interjected Mary, "I want you to tell me about some of the complications that followed Robert Gray's discovery of the Columbia. Yesterday morning you raised my curiosity about that."

Jason smiled and helped himself to some more oatmeal. "This is what happened," he said, after sprinkling brown sugar on the oatmeal, and covering it with milk. "Gray, of course, kept a log of his travels, but he did not publish it. So the world only learned about his achievements from the published journals of that busy Englishman, George Vancouver.

"Vancouver explored a lot and drew many maps. He gave names to Mount Rainier, Mount Baker and Mount Hood, along with many other places. He wanted to name that part of the area New Georgia, in honor of the king of England. As a result of his fame, the British give him more credit than they give to our Robert Gray.

"Finally, last year, President Madison asked for a copy of Robert Gray's log. Gray is now dead, but fortunately someone discovered that one of the owners of the Columbia had copied a portion of the log that carried the notations about the discovery of the Columbia River."

"And what about that wastepaper basket of Gray's niece?" Mary asked.

"She had the log and was using it for wastepaper."

"Using it for wastepaper?" exclaimed Mary.

"Yes, using it for wastepaper!"

"The Louisiana Purchase was a great bargain," Jason continued with additional fervor. "But when we latch onto the Northwest we'll get it for nothing."

"For nothing?" asked Elias.

"Yes. Neither Britain nor the United States is interested enough to claim it," explained Jason.

"Why not?"

"Too many bears and Indians." Jason stood up and opened the door. "Goodbye. Have to go to work. See you tonight."

Invigorated by what he had learned, Jason swung his ax harder than ever. Soon he was stacking a larger pile than any two of the men.

"What happened to you?" demanded Jeff.

"That Lewis and Clark book is really inspiring me," he replied. "One of these days I'm going to become a mountain man! Smack-dab, I can already feel the excitement in my bones."

All at once there was a searing flash of lightning followed by a crash of thunder. Then it began to drizzle. The drizzle was followed by heavier rain, and the heavier rain was followed by a blinding, drenching rain.

Turning toward the two-storied log house where he lived, Jason saw that it was almost the target of a cloudburst. As he watched, his heart began to pound. *He had failed to close the window, and the borrowed book was right in the middle of his bed! What would he do?*

Whirling on the men, he shouted, "You're dismissed! See you Monday."

Full of fear, he headed home. He paid no heed to muddy puddles. In spite of his new boots, he stomped through them as if they didn't exist. He had only one thought: He must save that borrowed book.

"Jason Lee," exclaimed Mary as he burst through the door, "you're completely soaked." Her eyes widened. "And you've ruined your new boots."

"I-I g-guess so. But I'm worried about my book." He wiped the water from his face. "It must be ruined." He nervously rubbed his hands.

"You mean that one?" She pointed toward the Lewis and Clark book in the center of the table.

Rushing over, Jason picked it up. It was bone dry.

"Oh, Mary, you've saved the day!" he shouted. He squeezed her so tight he almost cracked her ribs. "I was terribly worried." He sighed with relief. "That book belongs to Jeff's uncle. He's awful particular, especially about books." Jason thumbed through several pages. "What inspired you to take it off my bed?"

"I saw the rain comin' and so I closed your window. Then to be extra sure, I moved your bed to the other side of the room and placed your book on the table." She studied him from head to toe. "You'd better put on some clean duds and sit by the fire. We don't want our little giant to get pneumonia."

Jason's interest in the Northwest continued. After he devoured the Lewis and Clark journals, he studied dozens of other books until they became a part of his being.

Months and years galloped by, during which he began to shave and his voice scooted down an octave. In 1818, when he was fifteen, Illinois became a state, and the next year Alabama joined the Union. In 1820 Maine was accepted as the twenty-third state, and Missouri followed in 1821 as the twenty-fourth state.

During this expanding period, Jason's business continued to flourish. After a hard day's work on a hot June day, he was greeted at home by the tantalizing smell of buffalo hump-ribs coming from the kitchen. Peering at the stove, he asked, "Why the treat?"

"Well, you've been working extra hard; and I thought you deserved something special. Besides, it's your eighteenth birthday!"

"While Mary's gitten' things ready," said Elias, "I want to measure you. Every day your altitude seems to climb a notch."

Jason stood by the door frame where he'd been measured many times before, and Elias made a mark. Then he said, "Mmmm, you're now over six feet, three inches. If you keep growin' you'll make it to six feet, four." He rubbed his chin. "It must be that God has a special work for you to do."

His brother's last remark raised Jason's suspicions. "Are we going to have company?" he asked.

"Not that I know of," replied Elias.

Jason returned to the fireplace, still curious. He knew that Mary had a way of doing little favors when she wanted something extra. *But what could that little extra be?* He searched his mind but could think of nothing.

3
A Double Dare

The table was loaded with the best Mary could prepare. There was a heaping platter of buffalo hump-ribs and three dishes of vegetables, including one mountained high with creamy mashed potatoes. Its crater swam with fresh butter. In addition, there was coffee, pie and a berry dessert. Best of all, there was an enormous gravy boat filled with brown gravy.

Jason's suspicions increased when Elias wedged a pair of new sentences into the center of his normal prayer of asking the Lord to bless the food. "And, Lord," he intoned, "be with dear Brother Hicks as he starts the revival meetin' in our church tomorrow. May it be that many needy souls will be saved."

So this was the secret! Jason clenched his fists under the table, but managed to keep still. After all, the only thing better than buffalo rib steak was more buffalo rib steak.

Jason finished his third helping of potatoes and buffalo and two helpings of dessert and was enjoying his second cup of coffee. Elias coughed and then faced

him. ''Jason, will you be a-goin' with us to the meetin'
tomorrow? Brother Hicks is a real man of God.''

''I'll go once if you'll promise me one thing,''
replied Jason promptly.

''And what's that?'' asked Mary and Elias together.

''If you promise not to invite the preacher over for
a meal.''

''Oh, we won't do that,'' replied Mary in a
confident tone. ''Brother Hicks is stayin' with the
Millers. Tomorrow they're havin' fried chicken.'' She
laughed. ''All Methodist preachers like fried chicken.
Some of 'em even hog the drumstick!''

Jason followed Mary and Elias into the little
meeting house. Mary selected a middle pew on the
left and motioned for Jason to follow. By this
maneuver, Jason was trapped between her and Elias,
who blocked the escape route.

Jason realized that he was like a weasel in a trap.
There was no possible way to leave without creating
a scene. He gritted his teeth.

During the worship service they sang hymns of
Charles Wesley. The hymns reminded Jason of the
challenges of the Northwest. The staccato rhythm of
O for a Thousand Tongues To Sing transported him to
the foot of the tall waterfalls in the West; and *Hark!
the Herald Angels Sing* inspired him to think of the many
attractions that were summoning him to cross the
Mississippi and to keep plodding toward adventure
in the land of the setting sun.

The sermon by the rapid-speaking, pulpit-pounder
failed to keep his imagination from drifting to the
encounter Meriwether Lewis had with a grizzly bear.
But a final story gripped him. ''Some think that the
Christian life is an easy one,'' thundered the flushed
man as be both pounded and pointed, ''but they're

wrong. Completely wrong. The Christian life is the
hardest life there is. Mountain men I've heard about
think they show their toughness by serving the devil,
but it would be far more difficult for one of those men
to live as a Christian.''

At the conclusion of the sermon, the preacher
invited sinners to come forward, kneel at the
mourners' bench, and accept Christ.

As Jason watched several friends respond to the
invitation, he felt a lump forming in his throat; and
that lump expanded when Elias stepped out into the
aisle to make it easier for him to go forward. Even
though his eyes were filled with tears, Jason gritted
his teeth and refused to budge.

On their way home, neither Jason nor his brother
or sister said a word. Later, while they were dining
on leftover buffalo tongue, Elias ventured, ''Brother
Hicks preached a mighty powerful sermon.''

''Yeah,'' replied Jason nonchalantly.

''Are you a-goin' tomorrow night?'' pressed Elias.

''Nope.''

''Did you like his sermon?''

''I like what he had to say about grizzly bears.''

''Grizzly bears?'' Elias lifted an eyebrow.

''I was reminded of the face-to-face affair
Meriwether Lewis had with a bear.''

''Tell me that story.''

''I know it so well I can quote a lot of what he wrote.
You see, Lewis shot a buffalo; and while he was
watching it die he forgot to reload his gun. Then a
huge grizzly showed up. Here are his words: 'He
pitched at me, open-mouthed and at full speed, I ran
about 80 yards and found he gained on me fast, I then
ran into the water when the idea struck to get into
such depth that I could stand, and he would be obliged
to swim, and that I could defend myself.' He planned

to use a spear-pointed weapon meant for steadying his rifle when shooting. The moment he put himself in that attitude of defense, the grizzly suddenly wheeled and retreated.''

"That's a great story. Are you going with us tomorrow night? Maybe the preacher will tell some more bear stories,'' Elias teased.

"Nope! I'm going to my room and read about grizzlies in the Northwest.''

Like a freshly wound clock, Jason continued to employ more men to keep working. Years passed, and he grew a full beard which he kept carefully trimmed. He combed it every day. Then in 1826, the year Jason celebrated his twenty-third birthday, he was surprised one day, when he got home, to find that the table was already set.

"What's going on?'' he asked.

"The revival with Richard Pope is causin' such a stir it's hard to get a seat. How about going with us tonight?'' replied Elias.

Jason hesitated.

"Just this once,'' urged Mary. "Pretty please!''

"Sorry, I need to catch up on my bookkeeping. And I'm also dead tired.''

The next morning the sun was just beginning to warm the mountains when Jeff stepped onto the edge of the new land Jason had contracted to clear. "You're always first on the job,'' said Jason as he shook his hand. "And how was the vacation in St. Louis?''

"Great. I met a lot of mountain men who'd just returned from the Rockies. They were loaded with beaver, money and whiskey. Half of 'em were drunk. But one who was respectably sober told me a story about Jedediah Smith I plumb never want to forget.

"It went somethin' like this. One evenin' when Old

Jed was out trappin' beaver he met a grizzly face-to-face. The grizzly was ready and he warn't. Before he knew it the grizzly grabbed his head in its mouth and threw him down. Then it grabbed him in the middle. But fortunately Jed's knife and ball pouch shielded him a little. Even so, the knife broke in two. When friends got to him, they found that several of his ribs had been busted.

"Since none of his friends knew nothin' about medicine, Jed told 'em what to do. 'Go git some water and clean my wounds, then git some thread and sew up my head.' Since all of 'em were scared, they were afraid to help him; and so he pointed at two of 'em and told 'em what to do. One of 'em got some scissors and cut his hair real close to his scalp. Another washed his wounds real good, then another stitched him up with thread.

"After they'd sewed his scalp, they discovered that his ear was almost torn off, and so he asked them to sew that up as well. When they were all done, they put him on a horse and took him back to camp. Within two weeks he was well enough to go back to trappin'."

"That's hard to believe," Jason exclaimed.

"It shore is. But mountain air is clean; and then too, Jed is a clean livin' man. He don't drink nor gamble nor smoke nor chase squaws. He's a God-fearin' man. One man told me he wears the knees of his pants out by prayin' all the time."

"What happened to the grizzly?"

"I heered that a man by the name of Arthur Black killed it."

Jason shook his head, "I guess we'd better get to work," he said.

Jason was so excited about the Jedediah Smith story he could hardly wait until he got home. As the day wore on and the trees fell he kept rehearsing to himself the dramatic manner in which he would relate the story. Finally, he dismissed his men and hurried home.

At the table he said, "Preacher Pope may have a lot of good stories, but none of them are as dramatic as a story I just heard that came out of the Northwest."

"Let's hear it," said Elias.

Jason related the story as accurately as possible. But he added a little drama by showing how stolid Jedediah was while he was being stitched together. "The old boy didn't even flinch when his ear was sewed back together," he boasted. After Jason concluded, he nodded his head with satisfaction, and then he sarcastically added, "who in the Bible has a story like that?"

Stunned, Elias and Mary just stared.

Then Jason rubbed it in by almost snarling, "David and Samson killed lions, but which of them was chewed up by a bear, sewed together with thread, and lived to tell about it? Tell me, which one of them was as tough as Old Jed?"

"And where do you think Jedediah gets his strength?" asked Mary.

"I guess he was just born tough," shrugged Jason.

"I'm afraid that's not quite right," countered Mary.

"What do you mean?"

"Jedediah is tough because he's a Christian."

"What does being a Christian have to do with it?"

"He's tough because the Lord helps him." Elias quoted, " 'But they that wait upon the Lord shall renew their strength; they shall mount up with wings as eagles; they shall run, and not be weary; and they shall walk, and not faint.' That's Isaiah 40:31."

Jason only managed a faint "Oh?"

"And not only is Jedediah Smith a Christian, he's a Methodist Christian!"

"A M-meth-o-dist?"

"Yes, he's a saved, sanctified, and shoutin' Methodist. And, like you, he was raised in a big family. But you're ahead of him at that point. There were only fourteen of them while there were fifteen of us. You're also taller than he is. He's only six feet two." Mary laughed.

Jason frowned. "How do you know all of this?" he asked.

"Because I've been reading about him in some Methodist papers. I even cut a clipping from a paper that came last Tuesday. It's from a letter Jedediah wrote to his brother Ralph. I'll go get it."

In a moment Mary was reading:

"Oh my Brother let us render to Him to whom all things belong a proper proportion of what is His due. I must tell you for my part that I am much behind hand. Oh! the perverseness of my wicked heart! I entangle myself altogether too much in the things of time—I must depend entirely on the Mercy of that being, who is abundant in Goodness & will not cast off any who call sincerely on Him; again I say pray for me my Brother—and may He before whom not a sparrow falls without notice bring us in His own time together again."

"That's very interesting," replied Jason, "and it makes me want to become a mountain man more than ever."

After supper, Mary put an arm around Jason's shoulders. "Are you going with us to the meetin' tonight?" she asked.

"I'm afraid not. Am too tired."

At breakfast Mary said, "Jason, you should have

been there. Jack Thompson got saved! And you should have seen the smile on his face when he got up from the altar. What do you think of that?''

Jason replied, ''Last year the Russians gave up to Britain and the United States all their claims to Oregon as far south as the 54° 4′ latitude. What do *you* think of that?''

The next day Mary said, ''The meeting last night was wonderful. A dozen people went forward and Tom and Jill who had been planning a divorce fell into each other's arms and were reconciled. What do you think of that?''

Jason smiled. ''In 1819 Spain gave up all her North American claims north of the forty-second latitude. What do *you* think of that?''

On Friday morning after Elias asked God to bless the food, he said: ''I wish you two would stop playing that silly game.''

''All right, all right, big brother, I'll stop it right now.'' Mary smiled at Jason. ''But first I must report that many people are asking why you haven't been attending. They all told me that they're praying for you.''

''Tell 'em they're wasting their time. I'm going to be a mountain man,'' replied Jason. He headed for the door. Then he stopped, and all but snarled, ''I'm just as good as all of those hypocrites who go to church. I pay my workmen on time. I don't drink or smoke, and I save my money. Goodbye!''

Elias nodded his head with assurance. ''God's got his hooks in him for sure,'' he confided to Mary. He reached for his hat, pulled it onto his head and began to chuckle.

The congregation continued to pray for Jason, but his determination not to become a Christian remained as firm as ever.

A week later, after a sumptuous meal, Mary said, "Jason, do me a favor. Come with us tonight."

"All right, you've begged long enough and you are a great cook. I'll go with you tonight. But don't ever ask me again."

Jason took a seat on the right-hand side of the very last row. Secretly he had determined that instead of listening, he would plan his schedule for the month to come. But as Pope warmed up to his subject, he all but shouted, "Putting things off is inspired by the devil. Hell is paved with procrastination. *Today* is a wise man's day. *Tomorrow* is a fool's day."

Unconsciously, Jason sank lower in his pew, for he was acutely aware of the fact that he was getting older. During the invitation he felt God's presence in a most unusual way. Soon he was clenching his fists as he steeled himself not to respond.

The next night he tried hard not to attend the services, but he could not stay away. That evening Pope had a different approach: "Some of you are talented. You want to live your own lives. But the devil has whispered that if you follow Christ you'll have to forsake your dreams, and live a life of utter misery." He slapped the pulpit and his eyes seemed to focus right on Jason. "Do you not realize that God's plans for your life will bring you far more happiness than your own plans? Think of Simon Peter. He was a fisherman. He loved to repair nets, and to go out into the deep. He liked the smell of fish. Ah, but Jesus promised him that He would make him a fisher of men. And He did! And what did Peter do after he became a fisher of men? He gave up normal fishing with all its joys in order to have the far greater joy of fishing for men."

The preacher paused and pointing at one section of the congregation and then another, he solemnly announced: "This evening I'm going to throw out a dare. No, it will not be just a dare. Rather it will be a double-dare! Yes, a double-dare!"

As his listeners held their breaths he silently paced from one side of the platform to the other. Then, pointing again, he cried, "I want all those who are willing to give up everything—and I mean everything!—for Christ to come forward and solemnly pledge to the Lord and these witnesses that you surrender all for Him. Assure Him that you'll face poverty if He so directs. Yes, tell Him that you'd be willing to leave your loved ones and to become a missionary or—or a circuit rider—if that's a part of His plan for your life."

As the congregation sang and the invitation was extended, Jason wiped his eyes. Then he blew his nose. But he refused to budge even though many of his friends crowded forward.

4
About Face!

At home, Jason Lee was as tense as a bass drum. Pope's double-dare to fully surrender himself to Christ seemed terribly difficult. Didn't Pope know that he was only 23? And didn't he know that his entire life was ahead of him? Full surrender? Grizzly bear whiskers! While he paced back and forth weighing the cost, his mind leapfrogged to the Northwest. Again he envisioned snow-crested mountains, the mighty Columbia, waterfalls, rushing streams churning with salmon. And as he daydreamed about fighting bears, shooting elk, collecting pelts from his traps; and avoiding being ambushed by the cunning Blackfoot, he was convinced that he would have to forget all such adventure if he were to follow Christ. He shuddered.

Giving up the Northwest would be like losing both arms!

Eventually he went to bed, and fell asleep. In a vivid dream, he saw himself before a group of trappers ceremoniously hoisting Old Glory up a tall flag post. He announced that the entire Northwest now belonged to the United States. Next he had a vision of the future in which he saw a thick, beautifully-bound volume which told his own story. It was called *Jason Lee: Winner of the Northwest*. Shaken completely awake by the realistic dream, he was keenly disappointed that it was not true.

Now, as he studied the stars through the window and thought of the magnificence of God, he began to wonder if God really required full surrender the way Pope had preached. He wrestled with that devastating problem of surrendering everything, especially his longing to be a mountain man. Then he remembered the disciples of Jesus. *All of the twelve with the single exception of Judas, had given up everything. Yes, everything!* Moreover, Judas, the one who refused to give up everything, betrayed Jesus, and then in unspeakable misery, hanged himself.

Suddenly into Jason's mind leaped Jesus' words, "If any man will come after me, let him deny himself, and take up his cross daily, and follow me" (Luke 9:23). Like a harpoon pushing into a whale, the thought pierced deeply. He pulled the blind down and tried to sleep again, but he could not keep his eyes closed. He lay awake remembering a conversation he'd had with Elias.

Elias had said, "Someday you will change your mind. By the way you're acting I think the Lord already has a hook in your jaw."

Jason smiled grimly at that memory. *Elias was wrong! God had not snagged him with a hook. Rather, God had snagged him with a harpoon!*

Nevertheless, he gritted his teeth and resisted the Divine call. His deep "mourning" continued several days and nights. Then, while walking along the highway, and meditating on Paul's statement: "Woe is unto me, if I preach not the gospel" (1 Cor. 9:16), he all at once made a complete surrender; and cried out by quoting Job, "I know that my Redeemer liveth" (19:25). At that moment he knew that he had been turned about face.

That evening he got to the meeting house early. While many were still on their knees praying for the services, he stood up and publicly announced: "I have become a Christian!"

Later, he set the facts down in his diary:

> *I had lived without hope and without God in the world, but now the Spirit which I had so often grieved, again spoke to my conscience, and in language not to be mistaken, warned me of my danger. I saw, I believed, I repented. I resolved to break off all my sins. . . . I saw the fullness of the plan of salvation, cast away my unbelieving fears — believed in and gave myself to Christ — and was ushered into the liberty of the children of God. I was NOW by my own CONSENT, the property of another, and His glory and not my own gratification must be the object of my pursuit.*

From the moment of his new birth, Jason felt better than he had ever felt in his life. The grass seemed greener, the air seemed fresher, the birds seemed to sing more sweetly; and because the load of guilt which had formerly tormented him was gone, he had new vigor and vitality. He was confident that his life was going to count, and that put a gleam in his eyes.

He was even able to chop more wood!

But what did God want him to do? That was his *new* problem. He prayed for directions every day. He searched the Scriptures, and the only answer he received was an assurance of his salvation, along with an assurance that he would receive day-by-day directions.

Jason tried to be content. But often as he chopped

wood, mended fences, and dug ditches, he became weary of God's repeated assurance: "Be patient. I have a plan, and you are included in that plan."

One day Jason approached Jeff. "What would you think if I became a circuit rider?" he asked.

Jeff sniffed. "I'd think that you'd gone plumb crazy. I have an uncle who's a circuit rider. It's a difficult life. His circuit includes seventeen preachin' places. He has to sleep in a different bed every night. One night Jake—that's my uncle—had to spend the night with a couple that had seven little children and only one bed.

"While Jake was a-wonderin' where he was a-gonna sleep, the old couple put the three youngest kids to bed. Then when they was sound asleep, they picked 'em up and put 'em on the floor. They did this till all seven of 'em was a-sleepin' on the floor by the fireplace. Then they said to Jake, 'Riverend da bed's now yours.'

"The next mornin' Jake woke up on the floor while the old duffer 'n' his woman was a-snorin' in da bed."

"Do you expect me to believe that?" grinned Jason.

"Suit yourself." Jeff laughed and rubbed his whiskers. "Circuit ridin' is a tough business, and it don't pay much. A circuit rider even on a good circuit where he gets chicken at every house is fortunate if he lives fer ten years."

Jason smiled. "You may be right," he said. "But if God has called me to be a circuit rider, I'm going to be a circuit rider. I'm following directions."

In 1829, three years after he became a Christian, Jason Lee enrolled for a summer term at Wilbraham Academy. Situated about ten miles from Springfield, Massachusetts, the school had an attractive campus, and an enrollment of 165.

Jason was assigned to room number 13.

He had saved his money and was able to pay the tuition of $3.00 a semester, and board and room of $1.25 a week.

Dr. Wilbur Fisk, the principal, was deeply impressed by Jason, and arranged for him to be in his own tutorial class. Jason's broad shoulders, although somewhat stooped, were so impressive, he was soon placed in charge of a large hall where many of the boys slept.

Jason was overwhelmed by the number of books available; and he delved into the subject of circuit riders, remembering what Jeff had said about them. He devoured books on that phase of Methodism. In one he read: "A study of the circuit riders before 1800 indicates that half of them died before they were thirty. The allowance assigned each man was $64.00 a year."

With a pencil, Jason divided that number by 52 and came up with the fact that this allowance worked out to $1.23 per week, or less than 18 cents a day. Even worse, each rider only received that much if he could collect it. Few of them ever did.

In another book he discovered that most riders were paid in kind, rather than cash. This author told what one congregation paid their rider during a three month period.

Jason almost gasped as he read:

Shoe leather and corn from Tullis' class. . . . $1.75
Bridle leather from Hardy's class. 62
One small pair of shoes from Curtis' class. . 1.00
One pair of shoe soles from Lower's class. . .   .50
Two and a half yards of linsey from Alley's
    class. 1.25

In addition to the above and several other items, $16.78 had been raised.

After marking the place in the book with a slip of paper, Jason hurried over to Dr. Fisk's office.

He showed the page to the principal and asked, "Is it *really* that bad?"

Fisk laughed. "Yes, it was that bad; and many times it was even worse. Before William McKendree was elected bishop, he preached for an entire year in the West and only received twenty dollars."

Jason nervously fingered the lobe of his ear. "H-how d-d-did he l-live?"

"God took care of him. God feeds the sparrows."

"Is it still that bad?" Jason asked.

"In most places no. But in new fields it is often just as bad, or even worse." Fisk smiled. "Do you still want to be a circuit rider?"

Jason stood up. "Dr. Fisk," he said, "I'm ready to do whatever God wants me to do. If God wants me to be a circuit rider, I'm ready."

"Then let's shake hands on that. You're the kind of man Methodism needs!"

Jason continued in school until June 1830, then he returned to Stanstead where he taught in the newly founded Stanstead Academy. Along with his teaching, he preached in nearby towns and villages. Since he did not talk about the Northwest as much as before, friends wondered if he had lost interest in that distant land of Indians, waterfalls, and mountain men.

Finally, on March 1, 1831, Jason explained what was locked in the depths of his heart by writing to Osmon C. Baker, a friend who was then attending Wesleyan University. He wrote:

I have not forgotten the red men of the West though I am not yet among them. Oh that I had someone like yourself to go with me. I think I could cheerfully forego all the pleasures I receive from the society of friends here, tear myself from the embrace of my nearest and dearest relatives, and go (as John did before our Lord) and prepare the way before you. But I am building castles in the air. No, no. That, I fear, will never be. "Not my will, but thine, O Lord, be done."

Day by day as Jason studied and preached, he sought to find the will of the Lord. To a friend, he confided, "I'm at the fork of two roads. One road leads to Canada, the other road leads to the Northwest. The one thing I know is that when God is ready He will show me what I'm to do in such a definite way that I will have no doubt."

By the fall of 1832, Jason's patience was near the breaking point. Not feeling any special direction, he got out a sheet of paper, addressed it to the London Wesleyan Missionary Society, and asked for assignment to Western Canada.

After mailing the letter, he waited impatiently for a reply. None came. Each time he went to the post office the postmaster answered in the same monotone, "Sorry Reverend, there's nothing for you."

The weeks dragged by, the leaves turned brown, and the snows came; and still there was no reply. *Perhaps*, he thought, *my letter was lost in the mail.* But each time he considered writing another letter, he had a curious feeling that he should not.

In the meantime, however, he continued preaching in the Stanstead Circuit; moreover, he was glad to be able to report the conversion of many of his listeners.

What Jason did not know was that a mysterious, and yet magnificent plan was being worked out that would utterly change his life. That mysterious plan included an unexpected death, a treacherous journey from the Northwest—and a strange request for a black book from some Indians who were called Flatheads.

5

Book of Heaven

In the far Northwest, Indians were puzzled by the white men they saw. These strangers who kept coming into their country from all directions were most unusual. They possessed a wisdom far beyond their own. Instead of dragging loads on the ground Indian-fashion, they had wagons with wheels and many other items of magic.

When the Indians first witnessed a wheel they marveled. In a way it was a simple thing, but it was extremely useful. It made moving from one place to another much easier. Why hadn't they discovered the wheel? One could be made by simply cutting a section from a log, and then carving a hole in the center.

The wheel, however, was just the beginning. White men had many other magic items. For example, they had a compass whose needle always pointed north, even if it were in a cave or in the darkest woods. And instead of canoes, the palefaces had big ships that could transport huge loads together with hundreds of passengers. Likewise, they had slender sticks which could be made to flame into fire by simply scratching them. And they had a vile-smelling kind of "water" which could burn like straw and produce light in a thing which the palefaces called a *lantern*.

Often as Indians from various tribes sat around their campfires, they discussed the white men, some of whom had Indian wives. During one of these powwows Rabbit Skin Leggings, a Nez Perce, stood up. There were eagle feathers in the long, black hair which streamed down his shoulders. A tongue of short hair hung from his forehead and reached the line formed by his eyebrows. He was clothed in a magnificent Sioux costume, and all eyes instantly focused on him.

"We have often discussed the white men," said Rabbit Skin Leggings calmly in his youthful voice. "But in our discussions we have failed to think about the black Book of Heaven which many of them carry. I have noticed that the palefaces who carry that book, and open it day after day, are better than those who don't carry it.

"Sometimes I think about Joe Meek. He doesn't have this book, and he is a very wicked man. He is always drinking firewater; and sometimes he kills our people. In contrast to him, I think of Jedediah Smith. Smith always has the Book of Heaven with him; and I've been told that he opens it every day and stares at one leaf and then another. And I've been told that he prays so much the knees of his trousers have grown wide and have holes in them.

"Jedediah Smith is honest, his feet walk straight, he does not drink firewater; and he never hurts our people. Why? Because he has the Book of Heaven!"

"What should we do?" asked Buffalo Horns.

"We should get a copy of that book and learn from its teachings," replied Rabbit Skin Leggings.

"But how will we get it?" asked Live Wolf, who was sitting next to the fire.

"We should send some men to the land of the rising sun and call on Lewis and Clark. Our fathers told us about these men. They came here to see our rivers, to study our mountains, and to make friends with us. They smoked many peace pipes."

"How far is it to their wigwam?" asked Buffalo Horns.

"It is a long, long way; and it will take many moons to get there. But it will be worth the trouble."

"Then I think that we should send some of our bravest men to get the book," concluded Buffalo Horns.

In time, Rabbit Skin Leggings and No Horns on His Head started out on the trip. Soon they were joined by four others, including some Flatheads.

It was a weary trip. Two of the delegates turned back when they reached the Rocky Mountains. But the other four, including Rabbit Skin Leggings and No Horns on His Head, continued on. They faced many hardships. They swam rivers, hid from hostile Indians, hunted for food. Once they managed to kill a buffalo. At other times they lived on berries and fruit. Sometimes they became so weary they were tempted to turn back. "My moccasins are almost worn out," grumbled a Flathead, whose head rose to a triangular peak just in front of his ears.

"Never mind," encouraged Rabbit Skin Leggings, "we will get there by the end of this moon or the next. And when we get there we'll see the Great White Chief and he'll give us the Book of Heaven. That book will tell us about the Great Spirit and how to pray to Him. It will also show us how we can become wise."

On and on they continued. They crossed the never-ending plains, climbed hills, rested in forests, made campfires. Occasionally they met trappers who were on the way to the Northwest. If they seemed friendly, Rabbit Skin Leggings mentioned Lewis and Clark, and let them know in sign language that they wanted to see them. The answers were always the same; "You must go to St. Louis. It is on the Missouri River." Then they invariably pointed to the rising sun, and said, "St. Louis is a long, long way from here. You must continue in that direction."

Approaching one group that seemed especially friendly, Rabbit Skin Leggings had a question: "Do you have the Book of Heaven?" In response, the leader showed them a pouch overflowing with bullets. Then he laughed. "We are not Christians."

Eventually the Indians reached St. Louis and were directed to General Clark's headquarters. When he learned the purpose of their visit, he arranged a place for them to stay, and secured an interpreter to help him communicate with them.

During their second call at his office, General Clark related to them the Genesis story of the creation of man. After he finished, Rabbit Skin Leggings said, "Thank you very much Great Father. We are glad to learn these things." He hesitated and glanced at his moccasins. "But could you now give us the Book of Heaven?"

"You come back tomorrow and I will tell you about some of the things Jesus said that are written in that book."

"But we w-want the B-book of Heaven," said Rabbit Skin Leggings.

"Come back tomorrow."

The next day the general outlined the Sermon on the Mount and told the parable of the Prodigal Son. At the conclusion, Rabbit Skin Leggings bowed to show how thankful he was. Then he said, "Great Father, that was very interesting and it has been good for us to hear. But we are still hoping to have the Book of Heaven, the kind of book that Jedediah Smith carries with him.''

General Clark flashed a broad smile. ''You come back tomorrow, and I will tell you some more,'' he said as he shook their hands. Then he asked, ''Are you getting enough to eat?''

''Oh, yes,'' replied No Horns on His Head.

General Clark reached for a basket. ''I have noticed,'' he said ''that your moccasins are worn out, so I had some new ones made for you. I hope you like them.''

The entire delegation showed their appreciation with broad smiles. Then No Horns on His Head said, ''Great Father, we want to get the Book of Heaven.''

''I'll see you tomorrow,'' replied Clark. ''Tomorrow I will tell you how Jonah was swallowed by a great fish and how the fish vomited him up on dry land and how he preached to the city of Nineveh.''

The ''classes'' continued for a long time. But never did General Clark or anyone offer to give or even show the Indians the Book of Heaven. The Indians, determined to be polite, stopped mentioning the real purpose of their journey.

During this prolonged period, two of their number succumbed to a white man's disease and died. Both Narcissa and Paul were buried in the Catholic Cathedral's burial grounds, and someone wrote into the church records only the burial of Paul.

Finally, the delegation returned to the Northwest, loaded with gifts, but without the book they had sought.

Jason Lee was at the post office still looking for an answer to his application to become a circuit rider in Western Canada. The postmaster said in his usual monotone, "Sorry Reverend, there's nothing for you." Then he hesitated, and added, "I mean there are no *letters* for you. But here's your copy of the *Christian Advocate and Journal*."

Jason folded it, placed it under his arm, and returned to his home. That evening after supper, he sat by the fireplace and opened it. He noted that it was the March 1, 1833 issue. Perusing it further, his face suddenly lit up, for he saw a letter from William Walker, a half-breed Wyandotte Indian interpreter from northern Ohio. Intensely interested, for he had heard rumors about an Indian delegation calling on General Clark, Jason concentrated on the letter. It read:

> *Immediately after we landed in St. Louis, I proceeded to General Clark's, superintendent of Indian affairs, to present our letters of introduction from the Secretary of War. He informed me that three chiefs from the Flathead Nation, west of the Rocky Mountains, were at his house and were sick, and that one, the fourth, had died a few days ago.*
>
> *Never having seen any of these Indians, I was prompted to step into an adjoining room. I was struck with their appearance. They differ from any Indians I have ever seen; small, delicately formed, and the most exact symmetry.*
>
> *The distance they had traveled on foot was nearly three thousand miles. They said they had come to see General Clark, their great father, upon very important business.*

In that same issue, Walker told that this delegation had made the hazardous trip for one purpose: to discover the correct way to worship the true God. He also included a drawing of Ka-ou-pu, the one who had died and whom General Clark had referred to as Paul. The drawing emphasized Paul's flat head. In addition, it had a semi-circle of dots over the skull to show how it would have grown had his mother not shaped it with the board when he was an infant.

Other articles appeared in later issues. Jason read them all. Then a new article was printed which brought tears to his eyes. This one was allegedly Rabbit Skin Leggings' farewell:

> *We come to you from a trail of many moons from the setting sun. We come to you with eyes partly opened for more light for our people who sit in darkness.*
>
> *We made our way to you with strong arms, through many enemies and strange lands. The two fathers who came with us — the braves of many winters — we leave here to sleep by your great wigwam. They were tired in their journey of many moons, and their moccasins were worn out. Our people sent us to get the white man's Book of Heaven.*
>
> *You have made our feet heavy with burdens of gifts, and our moccasins will grow old with carrying them, but the Book is not among them. We are going back over the long, sad trail to our people. When we tell them in our council after one more snow, that we did not bring the Book, no word will be spoken by our old men, nor by our young braves. One by one they will rise up and go out in silence. Our people will die in darkness, and they will go on the long path to other hunting grounds. No white man will go with them, and no Book of Heaven will make the way plain. We have no more words — farewell.*

After wiping his eyes, Jason got down on his knees. The invitation to evangelize the Northwest was as plain as the setting sun that was then painting the western horizon. "Oh Lord," he prayed, "the door is open. Speak to the right people and encourage them to go, even though the risks are many and some of them may never be able to return."

The Christian world's interest in the mysterious delegation increased by the day. Any fragment of new information about the Flatheads was seized by editors and placed in a prominent place in their publications.

One evening Jason noticed an appeal from Dr.

William Fisk in the March 22 issue of the *Christian Advocate and Journal*. Since Fisk had been the principal of Wilbraham Academy when he attended there, Jason eagerly seated himself by the fireplace, and began to read. Soon he was wiping his eyes and blowing his nose.

Fisk's words carried great weight, for all of Methodism knew that he was an extremely dedicated man. Although elected bishop twice, he had on both occasions declined because he felt it was not God's will for him to accept such a high honor.

Fisk's appeal was more than an ordinary appeal. It was a double-dare challenge:

> *The communication from the Wyandotte agent has excited many in this section with intense interest. I have proposed the following plan: Let two suitable men, unencumbered with families, and possessing the spirit of martyrs, throw themselves into the nation. Live with them — learn their language — preach Christ to them and, as the way opens, introduce schools, agriculture, and the arts of civilized life. Who will go? Who? I know of one young man who I think will go; and of whom I can say, I know of none like him for the enterprise. If he will and we have written him on the subject, we only want another, and the mission will be commenced the coming season. Were I young and healthy and unencumbered, how joyfully would I go! But this honor is reserved for another. Bright will be his crown: glorious his reward.*

After reading the challenge half a dozen times, Jason finally shuffled into his room. *Was he the young man to whom Dr. Fisk had written?* He had not yet received such a letter. He knelt by his bed and prayed for guidance. Then a rush of new thoughts overwhelmed him. *Was the Lord opening the way for him to be a missionary to the Flatheads in the Northwest? And was the door closing for him to be a circuit rider in Western Canada?* He did not know; at least he did not know for sure.

He paced back and forth in his room. In his heart, he felt like Paul at Troas. Paul had longed to go to Bithynia. Warmed by the Black Sea, Bithynia had an ideal climate; and would be an excellent door that could enable him to reach all of Asia with the gospel.

Jason crawled into bed and pinched out the candles. He squeezed his eyes shut but his mind returned to Paul. Like all Bible students, Jason knew that after the Holy Spirit closed the doors to Bithynia, Paul had a vision in which a man from Macedonia stood before him and said: "Come over into Macedonia, and help us" (Acts 16:9). He also knew that Paul had followed the stranger's request; and, as a result, Europe and eventually America were evangelized.

Could it be that Rabbit Skin Leggings and No Horns on His Head were to him what the man from Macedonia had been to Paul? As he thought and prayed about this, he had a strong assurance that indeed they were.

Feeling confident that he was being called to the Northwest, Jason fell asleep. But early in the morning he was stabbed awake by a disturbing thought: *What will I do if tomorrow I receive an answer to the letter I sent to London, and it tells me that I have been accepted as a circuit rider to evangelize Western Canada?*

6
Northwest Assignment

The moment he knew the mail would be distributed at the post office, Jason Lee stepped inside and waited. As he watched the postmaster sorting the various pieces, he became conscious that his pulse was speeding. He began to pace back and forth nervously.

Finally the postmaster faced him. Lifting his hands, he rumbled in his familiar monotone, "Well, Reverend, you didn't get anything. Sorry."

Relieved, Jason mounted his horse and rode away to fill a preaching appointment. Several days later he received a letter. Thoroughly excited because Bishop Hedding's name was on the upper left side corner, he staggered outside, slumped onto a stump, and slit it open. The single sheet of parchment informed him that he was chosen to be the first Methodist missionary assigned to the Northwest.

Almost beside himself, he reread the letter a dozen times. Then he thanked the Lord that his prayers were answered. It seemed definite now that God had chosen him to be a missionary to the Northwest.

But he was still puzzled as to why he had not received a reply from London. Then he found out that an answer was never sent because the Secretary had died before Jason's application had reached him.

Days later Jason was ordained by Bishop Elijah Hedding. Officially, he was now Reverend Jason Lee, Missionary of the Flathead Indians. His next problem was to raise money, buy equipment, and arrange to cross thousands of miles to his new field of labor.

Raising money to start the mission was comparatively easy, for all of Methodism had heard about the Indian delegation. A bigger problem was to find a dependable guide to lead the way. Then, providentially, it was arranged for Jason to speak in Boston on Friday evening, November 29. When he took his seat on the platform, he discovered that he would be sharing the pulpit with Captain Nathaniel J. Wyeth who, at that moment, was sitting next to him along with two Indian boys.

The boys were obviously from the Northwest, for each had a flat head. The head of the older one, who was about twenty, was decidedly flatter than that of his teenage companion. Glancing at Wyeth, Jason noticed a slender thirty-year-old. His receding hair was dark, and the sideburns that fringed his jaws formed a puff in the center of his chin.

When Wyeth was introduced, Jason heard that he was a Methodist and that he had formerly earned a living by cutting blocks of ice from New England ponds, packing them in sawdust, and shipping them to the West Indies. Then, during his talk, he learned how Wyeth had met a firebrand by the name of H.J. Kelly.

Kelly inspired Wyeth with the idea that Oregon

could become the most prosperous state in the Union. He envisioned cities, farms, dams, counties, and enormous ports that would be kept busy trading with the Orient. As the result of the pamphlet which he mailed out in order to inspire a few pioneers, 400 prospective emigrants volunteered. Unfortunately, he had no money. He hoped that Congress would foot the bill. Congress, however, wasn't interested.

Kelly never fulfilled any of his dreams. Nonetheless, he had inspired Wyeth, a volunteer, to make the attempt. Bubbling with enthusiasm, Wyeth enrolled twenty-one men to accompany him and attempt to make real what Kelly had merely planned on paper.

Wyeth loaded supplies and equipment on a supply ship in Boston Harbor, then directed the captain to sail around Cape Horn at the lower end of South America, head north to the Hawaiian Islands, and then sail northeast and meet him at Fort Vancouver. Wyeth and the brave twenty-one started out by land on March 11,1832. They crossed plains, rivers and mountains, and reached Fort Vancouver on October 29, but many died on the way. The ship failed to arrive, so Wyeth released the survivors from their contract, and they retreated back to civilization. Only eight actually reached their homes.

"What am I to do now?" demanded Wyeth, jabbing with his finger. "The answer is plain! I'm now gathering another group, and we will start out from St. Louis this coming April."

As Wyeth spoke, he kept the audience on the edge of their seats. "Aren't you afraid?" demanded a voice in the audience.

"No. Why should I be? We made mistakes on our first trip. We'll not make those same mistakes again. If a godless Joe Meek can survive, so can we."

After services, Jason made an appointment to meet

Wyeth in his hotel room, a room which he shared with the flat-headed Indians.

"So you've been assigned to be the first Methodist missionary to the Flatheads," greeted Wyeth as he warmly shook both of his hands.

"That's right, and I'm very excited."

"How are you going to get there?" Wyeth leaned forward and fingered his puff of whiskers.

"Right now, I don't know."

"Why don't you throw your lot in with me?"

"Is there room?"

"Of course! The only problem is that you'll have to be ready by the middle of April. Can you do that?"

Jason scratched his head and was silent for a long moment. Then he said, "Yes, I'm sure I can be ready. But how will we go?"

"I'll be shipping my goods on my brig, the *May Dacre*. It will sail for Oregon by way of the Horn. It will be crammed with books, farm tools, chickens."

"Around the Horn again?" Jason stared. How far is that?"

"About twenty-two thousand miles."

"That's almost the distance around the world!"

Wyeth shrugged. "That's the nearest way by sea. But don't worry, there'll be plenty of room for your things. As for my companions, we'll board a steamer at Pittsburgh and follow the rivers to St. Louis. If we can manage, we'll get to Independence, Missouri, by the middle of May. Then we'll be off to Oregon."

"And how will we travel?"

Wyeth laughed. "Depends. Sometimes we'll be in wagons. Sometimes we'll ride horses or mules. We'll have to swim rivers and we'll have to be careful that we're never ambushed, especially by those murderous Blackfoot."

"About how long will it take to get to Oregon?"

"Oh, maybe seven months if we're lucky." Wyeth chuckled. Then he added: "Brother Lee, we'll be pressed by hardships every day. Some will turn back. Some may die. Others may be killed by hostile Indians." He rubbed his chin. "You'd better think about it and do a lot of praying before you start."

"That I've done. I'm committed. I'm not afraid."

Wyeth held Jason's hands in a firm grip and peered into his eyes. "The Oregon Trail," he concluded in a low solemn tone, "is not for cowards or the fainthearted."

Jason Lee placed his hand on Wyeth's shoulder. "You can count on me," he said. "I'm not afraid of death." Then he thrust out his chin.

Turning to the Indians, he said, "I'd really like to know more about how you flatten your heads."

The older one began, "All with flat heads are not Flatheads. Most Flatheads don't have flat heads. Those with flat heads do not all come from the same

tribe. I'm a Nez Perce and my friend here is from Canada. Flattening the heads of children is popular with our people because they think it makes them fiercer warriors—and better looking.'' He spread his fingers on his head and laughed.

"But how do you do it?" Jason asked again.

"When babies are born their heads are pliable. And so after a new papoose is placed in its cradle, a flat board is attached to the cradle. The mother then squeezes it down on the baby's head. The board flattens the baby's skull.''

"But doesn't that hurt?"

The older Indian laughed. "I don't remember. But I don't think it does. At least not very much. My mother told me that the baby's head is not flattened all at once. It's done over a period of a year or two.''

"Do they *still* flatten heads?"

"Of course."

"Why?"

"For the same reason that white women squeeze in their stomachs and wear long dresses with hoops. It's the style.''

On Sunday, December 1, Jason again mounted a church platform. Facing an overflow crowd with the flat-headed Indians by his side and having been introduced by Dr. Fisk, he was at his best. A newspaper was wildly enthusiastic. The heart of its report placed in a prominent spot was:

> *He does not, indeed, depend on his ability to command success; but feels that he is pursuing the path of duty; and is relying on the promise of God.*

While Jason was completing his speaking schedule, he persuaded Cyrus Shepherd to resign his position as a schoolteacher and accompany him in order that he might teach the Flatheads when the new mission was established. At the same time, the Missionary Board made arrangements with Daniel Lee, Jason's nephew, to be part of the team.

Jason was amazed at the way all his hopes were fulfilled. Then immediately after a crowded church service, during which over two hundred dollars were raised for the project, his old friend Jeff approached. "Let's go out and have a snack together," said the smiling man with the red whiskers.

His voice was so serious Jason was a little startled.

Over a bowl of soup in a tiny cafe, Jeff said, "Riverend, you and I've been friends for years. You were the best employer I've ever had. You paid me well, and on time. It's because of my respect for you that I've come to warn you."

"About what?" Jason paused with his spoon in midair.

"About this trip you're gonna take with Captain Wyeth."

"You're worried?" Jason asked.

"Yes and no. I think Wyeth's an honest man. But—"

"But what?" Jason leaned forward.

"He don't have even horse sense. Only eight men returned from his trip to Oregon. Many died on the way. One who survived gave a friend of mine an earful. He said that some of 'em starved; and some of 'em got so tired they dropped dead in their tracks. But that ain't all. When my uncle who used to be a schoolteacher—I mean the one who lent you them books—heerd that you was a-goin' to move to the Northwest, he said that if you goes there you's crazier than a mule."

"Why?"

"Because the Northwest is just plumb full of

Indians, and mountain men. Uncle Jack is a student of Tom Jefferson. And do you know what Jefferson said?''

''What did he say?'' Jason had almost finished his soup.

''My uncle said that President Jefferson said in his *Notes on Virginia* that it would take two hundred years before we reached the Mississippi and another two or three hundred years before our civilization reached the Pacific.''

Jason laughed. ''I know you don't believe that, Jeff. You told me yourself that you used to help mountain men load up in St. Louis. That's on the Mississippi! And, besides that, Jefferson is the one who sent Lewis and Clark to the Pacific Coast in 1803.''

''You mean you think Uncle Jack just invented that story?'' he asked.

''No, of course not. But when Jefferson wrote that, he was mistaken. Nonetheless, he was a wise man. He sent Lewis and Clark to the Pacific even though he had never been any farther west than Harper's Ferry. That expedition helped turn the eyes of the world onto the Northwest. God works in mysterious ways, Jeff. He knows what He's doing!''

Jeff signaled the waiter. ''Now bring us some buffalo hump-ribs,'' he ordered.

''Buffalo hump-ribs!'' exclaimed Jason. ''You're getting generous.''

Jeff smiled. ''I just don't want you to ruin your life.''

Jeff cut a generous piece of rib and while he spread a touch of mustard on it, he said, ''Let's just suppose that you do get to Oregon. What good would you be able to accomplish?''

''I'd preach and teach the Flatheads to live properly.''

"But you'd never succeed," Jeff objected.

"Why not?"

"Indian culture is completely different than our culture. Do you know how the Nez Perce believe they came into existence?"

"No, tell me."

"They say that a long time ago when the world was new, a terrible monster came into the land of Winding Waters. He tramped through forests, knocked trees flat, slurped up lakes, and ate all the birds and animals which he saw. Then he seized Coyote, who was warming himself by the fire, and swallowed him in one gulp. Coyote, however was smart. He had grabbed a burning coal from the fire; and while he was in the monster's stomach he used it to burn a hole through his skin and escape.

"The monster was now in terrible pain; and as he writhed and bellowed in agony, he shed great drops of blood. The moment those drops of blood touched the earth they turned into Indians."

"That's an interesting story," commented Jason without even smiling.

"But if the Indians believe such nonsense, how will you ever persuade them to accept the Christian gospel?" asked Jeff.

"Their story doesn't bother me," scoffed Jason. "It's quite imaginative. It's a work of genius. If the Nez Perce were clever enough to invent that story, they are quite capable of learning other things."

Caught off guard, Jeff stared in silence. But he quickly regained his composure. Then, a but-listen-to-this smile circled his face. "The Northwest is havin' a hard time these days. Even mountain men are in trouble. For years they got rich sellin' beaver pelts. There was a big demand for beaver pelts because they were turned into hats. But now silk hats have taken their place and the demand for beaver has almost disappeared. The result is that some of the meanest mountain men have become meaner than ever. I just heered a new story about Joe Meek.''

"What's that?" asked Jason eagerly. He helped himself to a slice of buffalo.

"It seems that Old Joe and some of his friends got into a fight with the Injuns. Durin' the scrap a mountain man was killed. After the Injuns had skedaddled, one of the men turned the dead man on his stomach. Then he and his hardhearted cronies used his back as a table. They shuffled their cards on it for a game of poker." Jeff rubbed his whiskers.

"Do ya' know what Joe Meek did?"

"What?"

"Joe was so upset he got up and walked away. Some said he cried. Now when things get so bad that even Joe Meek cries, they must be pretty bad. Yes, pretty bad. Take it from me, Preacher, you could get a revival a-goin' in the bad place before you could get one a-goin' in the Northwest!''

"On the other hand," replied Jason, "that's encouraging."

"Encouragin'! How?"

"It shows that Joe Meek has a tender place in his heart. Anyone who's capable of being ashamed of himself has great possibilities!''

"What do you mean?"

"I mean that when a person who has refused to accept Christ can listen to the gospel and not be ashamed of himself he's in a pretty bad fix.''

Jeff stood up. "Hold it now, Preacher, you've started to meddle!" Then he smiled. "I came all the way over here to warn you; but if you're determined to risk your life, there's nothin' that I can do about it." He held out his hand. Then he peered sharply at Jason and asked, "What is it that makes you so fearless?"

"I'm not really fearless, Jeff. But I do know that the Lord has promised never to forsake me. Yes, I know that things will be tough. But they were also tough for Paul. Paul is my model. Let me read to you what happened to him." Jason opened his New Testament and read:

> Of the Jews five times received I forty stripes save one. Thrice was I beaten with rods, once was I stoned, thrice I suffered shipwreck, a night and a day I have been in the deep; in journeyings often, in perils of water, in perils of robbers, in perils of mine own countrymen, in perils by the heathen, in perils in the city, in perils in the wilderness, in perils in the sea, in perils among false brethren; in weariness and painfulness, in watchings often, in hunger and thirst, in fastings often, in cold and nakedness (2 Cor. 11:24-27).

"If God enabled Paul to do that, He will also enable me to do the work in the Pacific Northwest," concluded Jason.

Jeff laughed. Then, looking wise, he added, "But you may face some perils even Paul never faced."

"For example?"

"Grizzly Bears. Blackfoot. Tomahawks. Scalping knives. Disease. Mountain men who don't want the Injuns to be helped. The British who want the Northwest to be a part of Canada—and a few other things."

"Even so, I'm prepared," replied Jason.

They both laughed and shook hands again.

7

Gateway to Adventure

During the second week of March, following months of frantic preparation, and speaking at innumerable churches in order to raise money for the Flathead Mission, Jason, together with nephew Daniel, boarded a steamboat at Pittsburgh and headed for Cincinnati, 450 miles away.

The deep-throated whistle groaned several times, the anchor was lifted, and the ship eased slowly into the center of the river and headed south on its long journey to the Queen City. Having unpacked his things and arranged the cabin to his liking, Jason climbed the steps, and joined Daniel by the rail on the upper deck.

"We're on our way," he exulted, slapping Dan's shoulder. "A dream is being fulfilled. By early winter we'll be in the land of the Flatheads, grizzly bears, great rivers, tall forests, snowcapped mountains—and maybe early death."

"Are you worried?" asked Dan.

"No." Jason's eyes scanned the magnificent

farmland they were passing. "I feel like Paul when he sailed to Philippi. Still, I am concerned. I'll never forget when I told my five brothers, and four sisters Godspeed. All of us wept, especially Mary and Elias. And several of them assured me that they'd never see me again."

Alone in his cabin, the optimistic faith Jason expressed to Daniel skidded a little. It was great to think that he was like Paul on the way to Philippi. But he also remembered that Paul made another trip, this one to Jerusalem. And as a result of that trip, he was seized and finally executed. *Would this be his fate?* He opened his New Testament to Paul's ecstatic passage in 2 Corinthians 11:24-27. As he reread it, he smiled. At least there was no chance that he would suffer shipwreck as he walked across the plains and followed mountain passes!

He came to the phrase, "in perils among false brethren." What did that mean? *Could other followers of Christ be a peril to him?* He snapped his New Testament shut, and tried to convince himself that such an idea was impossible. Selecting a new pen, he addressed a letter to Osmon C. Baker. Summoning confidence, he wrote:

"My dear brother, I go as Paul went to Jerusalem, bound in spirit, not knowing what will befall me there; but, thank God, I have had but very few anxious thoughts about everything else, except being faithful in the cause of Christ—that is enough—that is all."

Jason tried to remain optimistic, but often as the ship followed the coils of the river, he remembered that of the twenty-one fully armed men who left for Oregon with Nathaniel Wyeth, only eight returned. Those were alarming thoughts. But he was not afraid of death.

After a six-day journey, the steamship dropped

anchor at Cincinnati, and Cyrus Shepherd, the teacher, joined the Oregon-bound missionaries. Soon they were on their way again. They stopped at Louisville, Kentucky, where Jason gave a missionary address, then continued on to St. Louis, Missouri. Here, Jason asked Shepherd to precede them to Independence. "That's *the* gateway to Oregon," he explained. "Assemble our equipment, and assure Wyeth that we're on our way. We'll remain here so that I can visit with General Clark and speak in the churches. Clark has more knowledge of Oregon than anyone. And he's the one who entertained the Indian delegation. It's important that I see him."

"How do you know he's here?" asked Shepherd.

"I don't." Jason laughed. "I'll take a chance. The Lord is with us!"

After the Lees helped Shepherd board the *Ioway* for his three-hundred-mile westward trip to Independence on the Missouri River, Jason asked a man for directions to the office of General Clark.

Rising to his feet, redheaded General William Clark reached for Jason's hand, and led him to a chair. "So you're going to be the first missionary to Oregon!" he exclaimed. "That's wonderful. Now tell me what you think of our great city, St. Louis."

"The city's full of surprises," ventured Jason.

"For example?" Clark's eyes sparkled in his thin face.

"Instead of putting yokes on the necks of oxen, they put them in front of their horns. And when I asked a gentlemen for directions to your office, he answered in French. Then I went up to another, and he replied in Spanish. Finally, I approached a slave; and, believe it or not, he spoke in French."

The General chuckled. "You see, St. Louis is an old, old city. It was here even before the Union was established. Thus far, we've been under three flags: Spanish, French, and now American.'' He stood up and pointed to a trio of flags on the wall. ''Each nation left an imprint. The Spanish put ox yokes in front of the horns of their oxen. And the French influenced our cooking.''

Not wanting to miss a word, Jason leaned forward.

''In 1764 a trading post was first established here. It was dubbed Laclede's Village after one of the founders, and that was a good name; for Laclede was in the fur trade, and the main purpose of his few buildings was to create a terminal for that business. Laclede was a Frenchman and he later named the city St. Louis in honor of the king of France, Louis XV. That was a strange thing for him to do; for, by then all this territory west of the Mississippi had been turned over to Spain by a treaty. Nonetheless, the name stuck because a large part of the population was French.

''Then, in 1800, Spain returned the land to France. The French only kept it for three years. In 1803 Napoleon sold this entire area, plus a lot more to the United States in the Louisiana Purchase.'' He smiled and took a deep breath. ''St. Louis then became the capital of Upper Louisiana, which has since been renamed the Territory of Missouri.''

''What is the city's population now?'' asked Jason.

Clark smiled. ''It's well over 6000. St. Louis is destined to become one of the great cities in America.'' He stroked his forehead. ''Ah, but wouldn't you like some tea?''

Without waiting for an answer, he clapped his hands.

A moment later, a slave shuffled into the room.

''Bring us some tea and a bit of chocolate cake,'' ordered the General.

Over a cup of tea, Jason asked one of the questions that had been burning in his heart for a long time. "General, why is it that neither the United States nor Great Britain claim Oregon? That's valuable territory."

"You're right. It's extremely valuable territory. And the reasons we don't claim it are a little complex. You see, since as far back as 1670 the Hudson's Bay Company, a British firm, has been hunting beaver there and buying beaver pelts from the Indians. They make a great profit, but about ten years ago Parliament became unhappy because the company was a monopoly. Also, the British had lost their taste for empire. So they made an agreement with the United States that the area was to remain free and open to citizens of both countries."

Clark got up and pointed to a map. "In time, either the United States or Great Britain will claim it," he concluded.

"Which country do you think it will be?" asked Jason.

"I think it will probably be claimed by the country that has the most people living there at the time. Right now the British are in the majority. The most powerful man among them is the Irishman, Dr. John McLoughlin. He heads the Hudson's Bay Company in Oregon. His word is almost law. You'll have to get along with him."

Jason stood up. "One more question. What did you think of the Flathead delegation?"

"Oh, they were wonderful men; and they were very sincere. Would you like to see the graves of the two who were buried here?"

"I certainly would!" replied Jason eagerly.

"I'll draw you a map that will show you how to get there."

Jason wanted to ask why the General had not given the Indians the Book of Heaven, but since he felt that would not be diplomatic, he merely held out his hand and thanked him for the tea and the interview.

As he stood before the graves of Narcissa and Paul in the Catholic Cathedral's burial grounds, his eyes overflowed with tears. Once again the final words of Rabbit Skin Leggings' farewell came to him:

You have made our feet heavy with burdens of gifts, and our moccasins will grow old with carrying them, but the Book is not among them. We are going back over the long sad trail to our people. When we tell them in our council after one more snow, that we did not bring the Book, no word will be spoken by our old men, nor by our young braves. One by one they will rise up and go out in silence. Our people will die in darkness, and they will go on the long path to other hunting grounds. No white man will go with them, and no Book of Heaven will make the way plain. We have no more words — Farewell.

Lingering by the graves, Jason prayed that the Lord would help him to be faithful to the task which He had assigned to him. Dabbing at his eyes, he thought about what he would say at the missionary meeting where he was to speak on Monday evening, April 7.

On the following Tuesday, Jason and Daniel mounted their horses and headed for Independence, Missouri, 300 miles away. It required nearly two weeks of hard riding to get there.

When they arrived, they found that Independence, the gateway to the Oregon Trail, was alive with mountain men, traders, Indians, wagons, and horses. On being informed that he would need at least five men to make the trip possible, both Lees interviewed prospects until they found two more men who suited them.

One day they watched a veteran teaching a

tenderfoot how to pack a mule.

"Gettin' a mule ready ain't the easiest thing in the world," lectured the survivor of many trips. "All mules is as stubborn as the devil hisself. Now thar ain't but one way to pack a mule, and that's the right way. Watch." He picked up the cinch belt, and waved it before the tenderfoot. "This belt has to be tight and I mean tight! Now let me watch *you* put it on."

The tenderfoot stepped in front of the mule, and the mean-looking critter stomped on his foot. "That's lesson number one," said the teacher after squirting a stream of tobacco juice. "When you work with mules you have to be keerful. Try again."

This time the mule whirled and kicked with both feet. Miraculously, the tenderfoot dodged them. "See what I told you," commented the instructor. "You gotta watch both ends of a mule!" He pointed to a deep scar on his forehead. "Got that from Jackson. That ornery brute would have killed me if I'd been an inch closer. Both ends of these critters is dangerous!"

After several tries the greenhorn got the cinch belt in place.

"Now pull it tight."

The tenderfoot pulled the belt up two more holes.

"That ain't tight 'nuff. Pull it tighter."

Puffing hard, he tightened it an extra notch.

"Now since you ain't a-gonna be ridin' this mule, I'll put on the packsaddle, and show you how to pack him." He methodically harnessed him with the additional straps. Then he carefully balanced the load. "If you don't balance the weight on each side, it'll slip off and then you'll be in real trouble, especially if you're in a tight mountain pass."

He finished loading the mule, and said, "The ornery critter's ready fer Oregon."

At the word *Oregon*, the mule suddenly began to shiver and shake like a dog emerging from a river. Soon his load was on the ground and he was celebrating by kicking his heels in all directions.

The instructor quickly grabbed the halter and forced him into submission. "See, what I told you," he stormed. "You didn't pull the cinch belt tight enough."

"But I did."

"No, you didn't. That ornery cuss pulled a trick on you. I seed 'im a-doin' it. But I thought you needed to l'arn a lesson, and so I didn't say nothin'. You see, each time you pulled the cinch strap, he took a deep breath so that the strap would be loose. What you gotta do is to wait till he lets go of his breath, and then pull. Mules are smart, but you gotta be smarter."

"Watch me and I'll show you how to do it." Skillfully he replaced the cinch strap. Then, just before he pulled it tight, he thumped the mule in the belly with his knee. Before it could suck in its breath again, he jerked the strap five notches tighter than it had been. While reloading, he said, "You must narrow 'em by kickin' 'em in the gut just before you pull the strap. My pappy taught me that. Now grab the halter and lead him over there." He pointed to a tree fifty yards away.

Wary of being bitten, the tenderfoot gingerly followed instructions. The mule refused to budge. "You'll have to give him a few whacks on the behind," coached the teacher.

None of the whacks moved him.

"Whack him a little harder."

This time the tenderfoot's whip almost whistled.

Again the mule refused to budge. The instructor held his sides and laughed. "That mule is takin' advantage of you! But don't shoot 'im. Mules cost

money! Watch me. I'll l'arn you what to do."
Keeping to the side in order to avoid the mule's hoofs,
he gave its tail a tight twist. When that didn't work,
he took a pair of pliers from his pocket, clamped them
onto its ear and began to twist.

This time there was a response.

The trainer clapped his hands. "Friend of mine gets
'em started by chewin' their ears. Not me. I prefer
terbakker!" He laughed. "Another buddy built a fire
under his mule. The mule got even by pullin' the
wagon over the fire and then balkin' again. Whole
wagon went up in smoke. Served him right. Fire
generally ain't the answer. Of course, there are
times!" He smiled and looked wise. Then he added,
"Some get 'em started by lighten' the load. Others
hold a carrot out in front of 'em. There are all sorts
of ways to git a mule a-goin'. You gotta find ways
that suits you. Each mule is different."

"Excuse me," blurted the tenderfoot, throwing the
halter down as if it were a snake, "I've decided to
go back to Ohio. Mules are too tough for me. I'd
rather teach children."

Shepherd had assembled the luggage the missionary
group would need on their trip and after they reached
Oregon. But Jason was convinced that they would also
need a few spare horses—and some cows. So he went
to the market and purchased the finest ones he could
afford.

By Sunday, April 27, the missionaries and their two
assistants, along with Wyeth and his assistants, were
packed and ready to go. Each man had a rifle, a
powder horn, a leather pouch filled with bullets, and
a useful knife. Although they were ready to start on
their perilous journey, they decided not to leave until
the next day.

Jason knelt by his bed that Sunday night with feelings of confidence mixed with feelings of fear. In his mind's eye he saw bleaching skeletons, painted Indians with tomahawks held high, and bloody scalps dangling from beaded belts. He thought of the eight survivors from Wyeth's first trip.

Realizing that he desperately needed to rest for the start of his journey the next day, he forced himself to turn his future over to the Lord. Soon he was asleep.

At ten o'clock on Monday morning, Jason mounted his horse behind his cattle at the tail of the long column of wagons, mules, horses, missionaries, and assistants. As he waited, he noticed that Wyeth's mules were loaded with every ounce of goods they could carry.

"I thought Wyeth sent all his things by ship," ventured Jason to one of Wyeth's men.

"He did. But since then the Rocky Mountain Fur Company asked him to bring $3000 worth of trade items. He'll deliver it to them at the Green River Rendezvous."

Jason wanted to ask more about the Rendezvous, but they were interrupted by Nathaniel Wyeth.

"Attention!" he shouted at the top of his voice. "We're ready. Let's go!" Milton Sublette, second in charge, then rode up and down the column and repeated the command again and again.

As Jason drove the cattle, he had no way of knowing that he and some of his cows, along with several of his men, would soon be achieving a series of firsts, and providing footnotes for history that would be read a century later. Nor did he realize that one of his "firsts" would be a very sad one.

8

The Oregon Trail

Now that he had left civilization and was in Indian territory, Jason nervously checked to see if he had everything he needed. Yes, his gun was in good shape, his bullet pouch was full, there was plenty of powder, his knife was sharp; his Bible and paper for letters were in the saddlebags—and he had a strong stake from which to anchor his mount for the night. He noted in his diary:

"May 3. I am sitting on the green grass with six Indians lying within three feet facing me and watching me. One is painted red." Then a few paragraphs later:

"There are *now* twenty Indians within six feet of me, and they are coming from every quarter. Who, *who* will volunteer to come and sound the trumpet of salvation among them?"

The caravan began to experience desertion.

With pencil, Wyeth scribbled in his diary: "May 5. We started with 3 less men, 4 having deserted and one new one engaged. Made this day along the Kanzas about 16 miles.

"6th. Moved along the Kanzas and made about 12 miles to noon and took observation, found the latitude to be 39° 38'.

"7th. Made about 15 miles and camped at Little Vermillion.

"8th. In the morning Sublette finding that his leg would not bear traveling, turned back. Made this day about 15 miles."

An Indian who spoke good English approached Jason. "Is it true that you are a missionary?" he asked.

"It certainly is!"

"And what Indians do you plan to visit?"

"The Flatheads."

The questioner turned away, but not before Jason saw the doubtful look on his face. While on a flatboat crossing the Kansas River, Jason wrote a letter to Dr. Wilbur Fisk. He planned to mail it by the hand of the wagoner who was returning to Independence. He wrote: "I am inclined to think that our journey to the Pacific will not be very arduous, though it will be long and wearisome. I sleep as sound and as sweetly as when in a featherbed. My health is good. I can eat anything. We have flour and bacon enough to last some weeks."

Leaders of the long caravan counted on being able to kill enough buffalo on the way to keep in fresh meat. But sometimes no buffalo were available. On the 26th Wyeth grumbled to his notebook: ". . . afternoon made 12 miles . . . still no buffaloe."

The next day he noted: "Saw 2 bands of wild horses. Killed one Bull so poor as to be uneatable." The next day his blessings improved: "Killed Buffaloe plenty." But in the same note he expressed a fear: "saw six Indians mounted today."

The sight of Indians here was frightening, for the

Plains Indians cared little for trapping. Instead, each tribe specialized in raiding other tribes; and all tribes enjoyed swooping down on the caravans, killing people, scalping them, and stealing their horses and valuables. All were expert horsemen.

Having crossed into what was to become the southern part of Nebraska, they struck "the main Blue" and camped near its banks. By the 17th they were in sight of the Platte, which had become a part of the Oregon Trail, since it follows a northwestern course. About twenty miles east of what became Grand Island, they reached this river and began to follow it. At some points, it was nearly a mile wide; but was so shallow and clogged with sandbars that it certainly fit its name, which meant in French *flat* or *shallow*. One man commented that it was "too thick to drink and too thin to plow."

After the caravan followed the Platte for four days, Jason was goggle-eyed at an enormous herd of buffalo covering an area about ten miles long and eight miles wide. He also viewed interminable green plains and herds of enormous-sized elk.

Often saddle sore, Jason wearied along in his saddle and kept his cattle together, the rhythm of his horse or mule seeming to mock him by sneering, "On-Wyeth's-first-trip-twenty-one-started, but-only-eight-returned. On-Wyeth's-first-trip—" Those words haunted him especially when he passed whitening skeletons. But at night, as he sat by a fire with the smell of coffee and supper in the air, and looked up at the stars, such discouraging words were pushed from his mind by Paul's statement: "I-can-do-all-things-through-Christ-which-strengtheneth-me" (Philippians 4:13).

The days on trail were not all humdrum.

Occasionally a couple of horses were stolen. Several

times both horses and mules got loose and had to be caught. Once a pair of grizzly bears was shot. And always there was deep concern about Indians who sneaked into camp. The perpetual question was: "Are they friendly? What do they want?"

Then there was the simple challenge of keeping warm. When there was no firewood, they learned to burn buffalo chips; and buffalo hump-ribs always proved delicious.

During the last days of May they continued to gain altitude. Jason began searching the horizon for the snowcapped peaks of the Rockies. As they slowly neared the foothills, they discovered that they were over a mile high. At that altitude their coffee boiled before it was as hot as they liked it.

On June 1, Wyeth triumphantly penciled in his diary: "Made 15 miles to Laramies fork. Forded this fork with ease and made 8 miles up the Platte in the afternoon. At the crossing we found 13 of Sublette's men camped for the purpose of building a fort."

The next day he noted a problem in his diary that had begun to plague them: "Left at Noon camp a bull and cow whose feet had worn out." Jason regretted the loss. He examined the hoofs of the other cattle and rejoiced to learn that they were still in fair shape.

Early on the 9th, Wyeth pointed and exclaimed: "Look! We've almost reached Independence Rock!"

Jason could see a dim smudge on the horizon. As the caravan continued forward, the dim smudge slowly began to take shape. "It looks like a bowl turned upside down," remarked Daniel Lee.

"To me, it resembles a half-buried mammoth egg. Let's hope it doesn't hatch just as we get there," replied Jason with a chuckle.

They finally stopped at the base of the strange projection that rose upward from a level plateau. "It's

called Independence Rock because Milton Sublette
celebrated the Fourth of July here in 1829,'' said
Wyeth. ''It's a good name. That rock means we're
now 838 miles from the eastern Missouri border.
We've averaged about 20 miles a day and are now
halfway to Vancouver. Considering our load of trade
items, that's great.''

When the caravan started to move again, Daniel
rode parallel with his uncle and Nathaniel Wyeth. He
asked, ''How are we going to cross the Rockies?''

''That'll be more simple than you imagine,'' replied
Wyeth. ''We'll go through South Pass, which
Jedediah Smith found one winter. We should be glad
we're not going through in winter.''

''Why's that?'' asked Daniel.

''Smith had a harrowing experience with that pass
in winter. He, together with Jim Clyman—he's the
one who told how that she-grizzly almost killed
Jedediah—wanted to cross the Rockies in the worst
way. But high snow that year made all the gateways
they knew impossible. Then they remembered that
a band of Crow Indians had told them about a pass

that was much lower than the others. But they couldn't remember just where it was. So the next time they met some Crows, Jim spread a buffalo robe and piled it with sand. Then he formed the proper mountain peaks. "Now show us where the pass is," he said. "With the help of the Crows they learned that it was just south of the Wind River Range. So they found the twenty-mile-wide gap that is South Pass."

"And they got through?" asked Daniel.

"Well, it wasn't easy," said Wyeth, "but at least the furious winds in South Pass blew snow away and kept the pass open. Jedediah and Clyman reached a stream called the Sweetwater, where they almost froze. Each man had to hang onto his blankets to keep from bein' blown away.

"In the mornin' they gathered twigs and tried to build a fire. But that hurricane-like wind blew the fire out. The winds had scared all the game away, so there was no food to eat. The men huddled in some willows for a day and night to keep from freezing to death, or losing their fingers and toes to frostbite.

"Early on the second day they wrapped themselves in buffalo robes and inched their way down the stream to where they found better protection between some rocks. One of 'em saw a mountain sheep up on the cliffs. He took careful aim, fired and—"

Daniel leaned forward in his saddle, trying not to miss a word.

"The sheep tumbled down the cliffs and landed smack-dab at their feet. Then there was a lull in the wind. They built a fire, and had fried lamb. It saved their lives."

Daniel was skeptical. "How do you know all this?"

"I've been over the trail before."

Wyeth led his caravan over South Pass in the fine June weather. At the summit they stopped to contemplate that they were on the ridge which separated the waters flowing into the Atlantic from those which find their way into the Pacific Ocean. They were on the continental divide. Some of the men shouted, "Hail, Oregon! Here we come!"

From South Pass they followed the Big Sandy River southwest to its junction with the Green River. Here, they turned south, and after two days of severe marching reached the Green River Rendezvous—a gathering where mountain men, representatives of fur companies, and Indians met in order to transact business with one another.

"We'll rest here for two weeks," announced Wyeth.

The men were tired, the animals were hungry, and here was plenty of water and green grass. More men arrived daily until there were nearly 600 of them.

Both the trappers and the Indians were as wild a group as Jason had ever seen. His eyes widened when he learned that after the trappers purchased clothes, they continued to wear them without washing or repairing them. They wore them until they literally fell off. But since the Green River Rendezvous also served as a yearly celebration, the trappers came dressed in their flamboyant best. Some of the fringe on their clothes were six inches long and longer. And each mountain man was crowned with either a beaver or coonskin cap.

They also decorated their horses with the finest ornaments they could afford. Jason gaped at silver-mounted saddles, saddlebags fringed with beads, tails decorated with eagle feathers, manes that were scrubbed and dyed; and necks and legs striped with vermillion and white clay. As he stared, he wondered what his relatives in Stanstead would think if they witnessed such a sight.

The Indians, also, took advantage of the occasion to show off to the best advantage. Noticing a fantastically painted brave, Jason motioned a trapper to his side. "How long does it take to get fixed up like that?" he asked.

"Wal, that depends," grinned the man. "It usually takes at least twenty-four hours. First, they take a sweat bath. Then they brush their long hair again and again, and put a touch of oil in it until it glistens. Next, they braid it 'til it's jist right. After that, they shake out their feathers until they look like they've just been pulled from an eagle—"

"What about their faces?"

"An expert does that. As I say, it takes at least twenty-four hours for 'em to git ready for a big shindig such as this. Injun girls also prepare to be as beautiful as possible when they're plannin' to come here. Look at that one over there."

Jason all but stared at the sixteen-year-old mounted on a horse. Her long straight hair, black as a gun barrel, had been carefully combed and parted so that each section hung halfway down her chest.

Her arms and fingers were heavy with rings and bracelets. Elaborate necklaces encircled her neck, and sparkling earrings winked on each side of her head.

Her beaded moccasins and leggings were made of the finest leather. And skillful fingers had covered them with elaborate and colorful designs made of red and blue and white beads. Her horse, likewise, had benefited by the touches of experts. In addition, a magnificently dyed blanket draped her slender shoulders.

"Why does she dress like that?" asked Jason.

"Because she's looking for a white husband!"

"But why would a man from Virginia or New York want to marry an Indian squaw?" asked Jason.

The trapper laughed. "Do American women east of the Mississippi know how to tan leather, or sew moccasins? And do they know how to make pemmican?"

Jason shrugged.

"Another reason trappers like squaws is that they're easy to divorce. That girl we're lookin' at is some punkin'. She'll have a man in no time."

The trapper stared across the crowd. Then, lifting his hand, he said, "Y'all 'ave to excuse me. I jist seed an old friend I hain't seed since the last Rendezvous."

During the week, Jason was fascinated as he watched the trading. He soon learned that "white men's things from St. Louis" cost up to twenty times as much at the Rendezvous as they did on the other side of the Mississippi. Sugar was $3 a pint; gunpowder $4 a pound; and red cloth for leggings brought $10 a yard.

As he watched and mingled with the crowd, a trapper inched up to him. "Some of the lingo I hear is beyond me," ventured Jason. "What on earth does 'which way does your stick float' mean?"

The trapper laughed. "That means: what do you think?"

"And what's the meaning of 'lie wolf's meat?' "

"Oh, that means 'be dead.' "

Jason frowned. "Where do they get such words?"

"Oh, it's a mixture of Mississippi River talk, Taos Spanish, St. Louis French, and a little Injun throwed in."

"Do you know Joe Meek?"

"Shore do. He's plumb full o' grit and the h'ar of a grizzly b'ar."

Jason laughed. "And what does *that* mean?"

"It means he's full of spunk." The man scowled. "He's also plumb full of the devil. Drinks like a fish.

Shoots Injuns. Lives with squaws. They say the only reason he ain't dead is 'cause the devil wouldn't know what to do with him.'' The trapper rubbed his whiskers and grinned.

"He's been captured by the Crows, lost in the snow, buried alive. Wunst he was out in the desert without food nor water. Pretty soon his tongue was a-hangin' out. Do you know what he did?''

"What?'' Jason's jaw sagged.

"It's unbelievable. But he told the story on hisself. 'I held my hands in an anthill until they was covered by ants. Then I licked 'em off. I took the soles off my moccasins and crisped 'em in the fire, and ate 'em.

"Sometimes when he was nearly starvin', and there warn't no crickets nor ants to be had, he and Kit Carson and their friends would vote on which mule should donate some blood. Then they'd cut a vein in his ear and drain off a pint. Quite a rascal, that Joe Meek.''

After the pelts were sold and purchases made during the first week, almost everyone stayed for another week. The second week was dedicated to revelry and fun. Jason had been told that God did not cross the Mississippi. And now, as he watched, he understood why people said that.

He stared, horrified, as a young mountaineer shot a whiskey glass off the top of a friend's head at seventy yards. But when a visitor told him that Mike Fink accidentally killed his friend Carpenter in this manner; and that Fink in turn was killed by a friend of Carpenter who shot too low, he walked away in disgust. He didn't want to think about the whiskey-glass game.

Jason was also shocked by a system of gambling engaged in by both Indians and trappers. Players were divided into two groups. Each side faced the other, and in the manner of Button, Button, Who's Got the Button, a carved bone was placed in the hand of a member of one team. Then they began betting on which fist held the object. While the hours sped, the size of the bets soared.

As betting continued, the team with the object tried to confuse the other side with chants made dramatic by the rhythmic beating of wooden staves. The frenzied gambling lasted all night. After losing their cash, horses, and even clothes, a desperate few gambled their scalps.

Liquor flowed. And the missionaries were disappointed to see that Wyeth got drunk along with the others. "I thought he was a Methodist," complained Jason.

"He is," replied Daniel. "He's a *backslidden* Methodist! He got drunk because the Rocky Mountain Fur Company broke their word. They refused to buy his goods."

At the end of the Rendezvous, Wyeth ordered his caravan to reassemble. "Tomorrow we'll head west," he said.

9
End of the Trail

On July 2, Jason and his men resumed the westward journey with Wyeth and his caravan. Three days later, they reached Bear River, and still later they came to Snake River country.

While trudging west, they happened to meet Thomas McKay, stepson of the fabled Dr. McLoughlin. Jason shook his hand. The next day they met another important northwesterner. This time it was the colorful Captain Benjamin D. Bonneville, who had discovered oil just south of the Oregon Trail.

On the 14th, they reached what the Indians called *Shawnt shawnip*—Plenty game. Lush because of the confluence of the Snake and Portneuf rivers, there were vast quantities of buffalo chips. Viewing them, Jason agreed the Indian name was correct.

"Well, Mr. Lee," announced Wyeth, his eyes glowing with triumph, "we've reached the place where I'm going to build my trading post. The Rocky Mountain Fur Company broke their word and so I'll establish a place of business here for myself." He motioned to McKay. "He knows this country like a book. He'll lead you to Vancouver."

Shocked, Jason finally managed to ask, "Do you mind if we stay and watch you build for a few days? We need to learn the ways of the frontier."

"Suit yourselves."

Jason and the missionaries watched as logs were cut, notched, and assembled into walks and buildings. The fort grew with amazing rapidity. On Sunday McKay took Jason's hand. "Preacher, why don't you conduct church services for us?"

"I certainly will," replied Jason eagerly.

Sickened by the drunkenness which he had witnessed, Jason had no difficulty in selecting a theme. As he faced some thirty whites and about the same number of Indians, he opened his Bible to 1 Corinthians 10:31, and read: "Whether therefore ye eat, or drink, or whatsoever ye do, do all to the glory of God."

Although the Indians could not understand a word, they remained attentive while he preached. Jason didn't realize it, but this was the first Protestant sermon ever to be delivered in the Pacific Northwest.

That afternoon during a horse race, a French Canadian was killed, and Jason was asked to preach his funeral the next day. Men wrapped the body in coarse linen and encased it in a buffalo robe. They dug a grave about a hundred yards south of the trading post. Jason noted the occasion in his diary: "I attended at 12 o'clock, read the 90th Psalm, prayed and then went to the grave, where I read a part of the fifteenth chapter of 1 Corinthians, and I also read the burial service which is found in the Discipline."

Once again, Jason had achieved a first—at least for the mountain region.

As the buildings neared completion, and the adobe

walls were laid, each missionary studied every move.
They were fascinated at the way the clay for the adobe
brick was poured into wooden molds, stacked in long
rows, allowed to dry in the sun—and then carefully
positioned with fresh clay onto the walls.

After a sufficient rest and learning time, Jason and
the other missionaries, with Thomas McKay and his
French-Canadians leading them, left for Walla Walla.
At a later date, Jason read about the fort's completion.
For publicity, Wyeth issued a bulletin about his new
trading post: ''I have built a fort on the Snake, or
Lewis   River   which   I   named   Fort   Hall.   We

manufactured a magnificent flag from unbleached sheeting, a little red flannel and a few blue patches, saluted it with damaged powder and wetted it with villainous alcohol. Its bastions stand a terror to the skulking Indians and a beacon of safety to the fugitive hunter. It is manned by 12 men and has constantly loaded in the bastions 100 guns and rifles. After building the fort I sent messengers to the neighboring nations to induce them to come in and trade.''

Jason was glad he hadn't stayed for the celebration. Another man's report said: "At sunrise the 'star-spangled banner' was raised on the flagstaff at the fort, and a salute was fired by the men . . . All in camp were allowed free and uncontrolled use of liquor . . . We had gouging, biting in the most 'scientific' perfection; some even fired guns and pistols at each other.''

Jason read the document and determined that when he built a mission it would be Christ-honoring.

The McKay caravan continued toward the setting sun. Day after day, Jason increasingly wearied of the endless miles of sagebrush and still more sagebrush. Suitable water was hard to find. Jason's lips began to crack. Then on August 12 the ready-to-collapse band camped on an island in the Snake River. With plenty of grass, and water available, they enjoyed a rest and felt optimistic. On a Saturday evening McKay dampened their optimism by announcing: "From now on, you are on your own. My men and I are going to Fort Boise to build our own supply depot.''

Surprised, Jason asked: "How will we find our way?''

''The Lord guided Moses, and he will guide you.'' McKay was unconcerned and a little sarcastic. ''By this time you've learned to overcome every problem of the trail. You'll be safe, and when you get to Vancouver my father will help you. He's a most generous man. Give him my regards.''

The next day the deserted missionaries gathered for worship. They leafed through their hymnal to Charles Wesley's hymn that opened all Methodist Conferences. Eyes moist, Jason, Daniel and Cyrus Shepherd joined hands. Then, while the stony-faced assistants watched, they sang to the tune of "Blest Be the Tie that Binds:''

> *What troubles we have seen,*
> *What conflicts we have passed,*
> *Fightings without, and fears within*
> *Since we assembled last.*

Jason read the final words in the eighth chapter of Romans. His voice choked a little when he came to the 38th and 39th verses: ''For I am persuaded, that neither death, nor life, nor angels, nor principalities, nor powers, nor things present, nor things to come, nor height, nor depth, nor any other creature, shall be able to separate us from the love of God, which is in Christ Jesus our Lord.''

Without a guide, the missionaries followed the Snake River until they came to the Grande Ronde River. Then they traveled south into its rich valley before continuing west again. While camping in the Blue Mountains, Daniel crouched low before the fire where Jason was frying a piece of venison.

''Do you think our missionary board ever worries about us?'' he ventured.

''I'm sure they do.'' Jason looked questioningly at him through the smoke, for he detected a hidden meaning in Daniel's voice.

''I've been wondering if some of them worry that

one or two of us might—just might—take up with an Indian squaw, in the manner of Joe Meek.''

Jason turned the meat over. ''What makes you worry about that?''

''I was remembering the time when one of the board members introduced you to Anna Maria Pitman.''

''How did you know about that?'' Jason asked.

''You told me!''

''Yes, I guess I did. Anna is a fine woman. We're about the same age, but I'd never consider marrying her.''

''Why not?''

''Because I'm going to remain a bachelor all my life. I don't think Paul ever married; neither will I!'' He removed the pan from the flames and set it on some smoldering coals at the edge of the fire.

As they talked, the sky filled with bright stars.

''I remember Anna well. She was the oldest of thirteen children. As each child was born, she had to take care of it. But as I said, I'd *never* think of marrying her, or anyone else. Dan, I'm just not going to get married.'' He took out his New Testament. ''Listen to this. It's found in Matthew 19:29. 'And every one that hath forsaken houses, or brethren, or sisters, or father, or mother, or wife, or children, or lands, for my name's sake, shall receive a hundredfold, and shall inherit everlasting life.' ''

After the men finished supper, they washed the dishes in the nearby stream, and then curled up by the fire. While the others were making sleep noises, Jason's mind switched to Anna Pittman. She came into such clear focus, he saw her straight black hair. It was parted in the center, and braided across the back-top of her head in such a way that her ears were exposed. He also noticed her dark eyes and heavy, dark brows. Eventually, while the yapping of a distant coyote drifted up to him, he fell asleep.

In the morning, they continued across the Blue Mountains, and kept plodding until they reached Fort Walla Walla on the evening of September 2.

At Walla Walla, they became the guests of P.C. Pambrun, the Hudson's Bay chief trader, officer in charge of the fort, and a Roman Catholic. Pambrun treated them as if they were his nearest relatives. "Make yourselves at home," he insisted.

While resting, Jason faced a problem. The way from Walla Walla to Vancouver was down the Columbia River. They could board a ship and sail westward. But at The Dalles they would have to leave the ship, walk around the cataracts, and board a second ship on the other side. They would also be forced to do the same when they reached The Cascades, another impassible obstacle.

"We can hire Indians to help carry our loads around The Dalles and The Cascades," noted Daniel. "But what will we do with our animals?"

"I'll ask Pambrun," replied Jason. "He seems to be full of ideas."

"Your problem is solved," replied Pambrun. "Leave your animals with me. When you get to Vancouver you can take an equal number of mine."

Jason almost gasped. "You are indeed, an agreeable man!" he exclaimed as he warmly shook his hand.

Pambrun smiled. "I always try to be helpful."

On a sheet of paper, Jason noted that he was exchanging three cows, ten horses, and four mules for an identical number in Vancouver. Again, he may not have known it; but the fact that he had driven the cows from Independence, Missouri, to Fort Walla Walla was another first.

The missionaries sat in comfortable chairs while sailing westward on the Columbia, and the conversation turned to Dr. John McLoughlin, Chief Factor of the Hudson's Bay Company.

"I remember discussing him with General Clark," said Jason. "Clark had a high opinion of him, and he suggested that due to the fact that the British firm, the Hudson's Bay Company, had been trapping beaver in Oregon since 1670, the British feel that they have a right to the entire Northwest. Still, they *really* don't want it. They're like a dog in the manger who doesn't like the oats but still refuses to leave."

"Then why doesn't the United States claim it?" asked Cyrus Shepherd, the schoolteacher. "With its rivers, fish, game and fertile land it would make a good addition to the Union."

"They, too, can't make up their minds whether they want it or not. General Clark told me about an agreement that the area from 42° to 54° 40′ north latitude was to remain free and open to the citizens of both countries. Maybe—" Jason paused. "Maybe we can help explain to those in Washington that the *entire* Northwest should be taken over by the United States. After all, it was an American who discovered—and named—this Columbia River!"

At 3 o'clock on Monday afternoon, Jason and the others in his party stepped ashore on the pebbly beach that fronted Fort Vancouver. To their surprise, Dr. John McLoughlin was there to greet them.

"Welcome!" he cried, holding out both arms.

As they proceeded to the fort, Jason kept glancing at his genial host, who was reported to be the most beloved and powerful man in the Northwest. Fifty-year-old "John," as he was affectionately called, had been dubbed by legend: King of the Columbia, Great White Eagle, Emperor of the West, Benevolent Despot, and a few other complimentary—and uncomplimentary—names.

Broad-beamed, with a fighter's torso, McLoughlin's straight white hair was parted in the center, and dropped like minature sheets to his massive shoulders.

A tall man of six feet four, a descendant of European aristocracy, he led the way with a firm step that indicated he was organized, knew exactly where he was going and precisely what to do in order to attain his goals.

"I hear that you're Methodist missionaries. Is that correct?" he asked in his booming voice.

"We are. We've been sent to evangelize the Flatheads," replied Jason with enthusiasm.

"Mmmmm. I'm a little worried about how you'll be able to reach the Flatheads." A tiny frown crinkled his eyebrows.

"What's the problem?" asked Jason as he nervously twisted the lobe of his right ear.

"We'll talk about it tonight at the dinner table."

As they neared the Fort, Jason observed that the large oblong enclosure was walled by upright logs which were sharp at the top; and that an elevated, octagonal bastion dominated each corner. Each bastion bristled with a cannon.

Numerous houses on the inside provided ample room for the hundreds of laborers there, as well as for the constant stream of guests who dropped by and stayed as long as they liked.

Comfortable in a well-furnished guest room, Jason stretched out on the bed. Closing his eyes, he prayed for guidance for his new work.

Later, entering the sumptuous dining room, Jason was reminded of some of the dining halls used by royalty in Europe. They were seated at an oak table, and Dr. McLoughlin requested Jason to ask the Lord's blessing on the food.

The dishes, Jason noted, were blue; and the table was loaded with hams, ducks, an enormous turkey, a large platter of venison, and all sorts of vegetables. The silverware was the finest that could be purchased in London, and there was a crisp serviette folded like a tower by each plate.

A waiter dressed in crimson livery stood at the door.

While they dined, Dr. McLouglin said, "I'm delighted that you've come. The Northwest desperately needs good men. Unfortunately, the history of white trappers and traders here includes some terrible episodes."

"It does?"

"Yes, they began when John Jacob Astor first sent some men out here for his Pacific Fur Company." McLoughlin paused while the waiter held a dish heaped with mashed potatoes at his side.

After helping himself and crowning his little mountain with brown gravy, he continued. "A group traveled by sea, on the *Tonquin*, which was commanded by a company officer, a ruthless man named Captain Thorn. As you know, under the law, the captain of a ship is in complete charge, so this group was in trouble from the time they set sail.

"Four other officers and Astor's partners resented Thorn's dictatorial ways. All five fussed during the entire voyage." McLoughlin helped himself to a slice of turkey. "The *Tonquin* had difficulty getting around the sandbar at the mouth of the Columbia. The sea was very rough, but he ordered five men to go out in a boat and make soundings. All were drowned. Then he sent another five, and three more were drowned. Finally he got around the bar." McLoughlin motioned the waiter to bring him the platter of venison.

Between mouthfuls he continued. "When Thorn anchored here at Fort Vancouver, he announced that he was ready to trade with the Indians. But he was not willing to pay fair prices, and he angered a chief so much that the chief shoved an otter skin in his face. Beside himself with rage, Thorn rubbed the hide into the chief's face, kicked him into the sea, and threw all his furs overboard after him.

"When the Indians returned the next morning, Thorn believed that they had been sufficiently cowed. But at a signal, they all pulled out hidden tomahawks. Only five of Thorn's men survived.

"The next day a surviving trader enticed the Indians back and dropped a match into the powder magazine to blow up the entire ship. Fortunately, Thomas McKay, my stepson, had a cold and was away when the ship sank. But his father was a victim. There is no need for affairs like that.

"Another white man by the name of McDougal was smarter than Thorn. When he feared that there would be a general uprising of Indians around the Columbia, he stood before a group of them and held up a bottle. 'This bottle,' he said, 'is full of smallpox. If I pull the cork you'll all get the disease and die.' "

McLoughlin grimmaced. "The Indians were convinced. They remained peaceful for a long time.

"I tell you these stories because I want you to know that we have to be kind and understanding with the Indians."

The missionaries exchanged glances. "But we wouldn't want to deceive them," said Jason.

"I know you wouldn't want to deceive them. Still, a person has to *understand* Indians in order to deal with them. I've been dealing with them for years and I understand them—and they understand me."

Jason wanted to ask about the Flatheads; but always another story came up. Finally, when it was bedtime, he brought up the subject.

"Yes, I've been thinking about it," replied McLoughlin, "and I have an excellent suggestion I think you'll like. But it's getting late. Let's discuss it in the morning."

10

On the Banks of the Willamette

After a sumptuous breakfast, McLoughlin nervously cleared his throat. Then frowning slightly, he asked, "Why do you want to go to the Flatheads?"

Jason related the story of the Indian delegation that had called on General Clark, and concluded with the comment: "The Methodist Church was moved by this to send a missionary to these people. And they were intrigued by their flat heads."

McLoughlin smiled understandingly. "Your board made a common mistake. Many people assume that all members of the Flathead tribe flatten their heads. This is not so. Most of their heads are shaped like ours.

"Head-flattening is practiced by many tribes, even by the Chinooks who live around here. I have a suggestion. Instead of going 600 miles east to the Flatheads, why don't you start your mission in the lush Willamette Valley?"

"B-but I came as a missionary to the Flatheads," argued Jason.

"True. Nevertheless, I think I have a better plan."

McLoughlin picked up a pencil and paper. "Let's study both the advantages and the disadvantages of my suggestion. First, here are some of the disadvantages of going to the Flatheads:

1. Being 600 miles from here you'd have a terrible time obtaining supplies.

2. The Flatheads are slowly dying out. They are victims of firewater, tuberculosis, and the Blackfoot Indians who love to raid their villages.

3. Flatheads, like most Indians, move about the country. They might be near your mission for a time; and then move many miles away.

4. It is dangerous for whites to live near the Blackfoot. Ever since Meriwether Lewis shot one of their braves, although he had good reason, for they were stealing his men's rifles, the Blackfoot have hated white men. They consider a white man's scalp a special treasure.

"Now let's consider some advantages:

1. If you established a mission in the Willamette Valley, the Indians would come to you. And that is important, for there are many small tribes, and they speak different languages. By getting separate tribes together you could help them to love one another, and learn the Bible together.

2. The soil in the valley is rich and you could show the Indians how to raise crops. This would keep many of them from starving when fish and game are unavailable.

3. You would be close to us and it would not be hard for you to obtain your supplies and mail your letters to the East.

4. If you follow my suggestions, I will lend you boats and supplies."

McLoughlin smiled at them, and then asked: "Well, what do you think?"

"We thank you for all of your help," replied Jason
thoughtfully. "But we'll have to discuss this with one
another, and pray about it."

During the next week the missionaries, aboard one
of McLoughlin's boats, searched the nearby country
to find an ideal location. Feeling like Paul at Troas
when "the Spirit suffered them not" to go to Bithynia,
Jason confided to his diary: "Could I know the
identical place that the Lord designs for us, be it where
it may, even a thousand miles in the interior, it would
be a matter of great rejoicing."

He pored over the 16th chapter of Acts. "Could
it be," he wondered, "that Dr. McLoughlin is like
the man from Macedonia in Paul's vision who said
'Come over into Macedonia and help us'?"

Pacing back and forth as he prayed, he wished he
could consult with the Missionary Board; but, alas,
it would take over a year for him to write and receive
a letter from them.

With unsettled spirit, he opened the pages of his
diary again and wrote: "Oh, my God, direct us to
the right spot where we can best glorify Thee and be
most useful to these degraded red men."

One day the ship landed on the east bank of the
Willamette, and Jason surveyed the area a few
hundred yards to the east. He was impressed. There
was a heavy grove of oak and fir trees nearby, a wide
plain just beyond; and the Willamette River meant
that they would have plenty of water and direct access
to Fort Vancouver a mere sixty miles to the northwest
by means of canoes.

It seemed an ideal setup.

Assured that he was being directed by the Holy
Spirit, Jason pitched a tent. Thus sheltered from the
weather, he and the other missionaries went to work.

Jason remembered: "We took the green trees and

split them, and hewed out boards for our floors. If we wanted a door, or a coffin, we had to do the same. We could not advance very swiftly, and we did not finish our house till after the rainy season commenced.''

None of the missionaries was a carpenter, but Jason was a master with an ax and they had memories of how the buildings at Fort Hall were constructed. Their first building slowly evolved. Toward the end of October, long before they finished, it began to rain. The rain seldom fell in torrents as it frequently did in Stanstead. Instead it kept drizzling day and night. It drizzled when they awakened in the morning; it drizzled and put out the fire when they attempted to cook breakfast. It drizzled when they smoothed and notched the logs. Soon, they became so accustomed to the drizzle no one even commented about it.

The story-and-a-half building they envisioned was to be 32 feet long and 18 feet wide. There were to be two rooms downstairs, four windows, a fireplace and a chimney. With a jackknife, Jason helped carve the window sashes.

The chimney was built of clay dug from the land and sand scooped from the river.

Each Sunday Jason conducted religious services in the home of a Roman Catholic, French-Canadian, Joseph Gervais, who lived about two miles from the ''mission.'' The congregation of retired Hudson's Bay employees along with their Indian wives and half-breed children, crowded the living room.

Even though only ten feet of the roof was completed, the missionaries moved in on November 3. They had no furniture except the cots they had used in the tent. Although he often had to wipe the drizzle from his face, Jason was supremely happy. He was doing the work of the Lord!

Soon, Indians began to come and watch what these strange palefaces were doing. Occasionally, some attended the services in the Gervais home.

By February 6, 1835, the first building was completed; and Jason proudly addressed a letter to his old teacher, Dr. Fisk. At the top right-hand corner, he enthusiastically wrote the return address: *Mission House*. Yes, they were making progress!

Over seven months later, Dr. Fisk read, in part: "We have three Indian children (orphans) under our care. One a boy of 17 or 18 years whom we got to take care of our animals, but his mother dying soon after, we were obliged to take his sister of 12 years. The third boy of 13 years who came here and asked by signs to be permitted to remain with us we could not refuse. We devote one hour each evening in teaching them to read and spell.

"I trust it will not be long before we shall have a flourishing school here.

"We shall probably cultivate 20 acres this season."

After reading of these happenings, Fisk read: "I have requested the Board not to send any more *single* men, but to send men with *families*. I have also advised Daniel's *chosen* to be sent as soon as possible. A greater favor could not be bestowed upon this country than to send pious, industrious, intelligent females."

Those were difficult times. Daniel Lee became so ill he had to go to Hawaii for a prolonged rest, and the others came down with the ague. In a letter, Cyrus Shepherd explained some of the opportunities and problems which they faced:

"The special providence of God has, already, seemed to throw upon our care three Flathead orphans; one, a lad of fourteen or fifteen years of age. The other two are about seven years of age; one is a sister to the above mentioned lad, and they are the only survivors of the family to which they belonged; to this girl we have given the name *Lucy Hedding*. These children came to us almost naked, in a very filthy state, and covered with vermin. The girl had no other covering than a small piece of deerskin over her shoulders, and a deep fringe of the same material around her waist. I made her a gown (though not a very fashionable one) from some pieces of two-cloth, which had been used for baling our goods.

"J. Lee cleansed them from their vermin so that they do not now appear like the children they were when they first came."

As the work grew, more space was needed; so they built a 15-by-32 addition to the house followed by a 32-by-42 foot barn. During those first months, there was a shortage of food. Not having yeast, they had to endure unleavened bread. Fortunately, their cows produced a little milk. Also they were able to buy peas from some settlers, and there was a supply of pork from McLoughlin's ship the *May Dacre*.

Jason found it difficult to preach to the Indians. For, after he mastered one language, members of other tribes came to the services and they could not understand all that he said. In his old age, Yakima Chief, White Swan, remembered:

> *When Jason Lee started to work, he sent ten Indians from place to place to ask other Indians to come to camp meeting, and all the different tribes came together. Then he buy dry salmon and other things for the camp meeting. That was the first time we saw wheel cart.*
>
> *In the middle he makes a place for himself to preach and read the Bible on a little table. He spoke through three interpreters.*
>
> *While Lee was preaching, the Indian chiefs sat smoking, not caring to hear the gospel. Three or four days while he was preaching all women and chiefs felt different just like something had melted and hot had come down, and they throw away their tomahawks and caps (war bonnets) and fall down and asked God to forgive them.*
>
> *After the camp meeting closed he showed them how Christ used to do and sent them two by two among the rocks to pray, and the Indians used to pray just like birds singing among the trees.*
>
> *Truly this missionary brought light to the dark place for the Indian.*

Lee soon learned *jargon*—an inter-tribal language developed by traders. By speaking it, he learned that he could preach to almost any nearby tribe and be understood. Some phrases he used were:

Mican tum-tum clush. (Your heart good.)

Mican tum-tum wake clush. (Your heart is no good.)

Alaka mican clatamay Sakalatie. (Your heart good. You go to God.)

Sakalatie mamoke tum-tum clush. (God make heart good.)

Hiyack wah-wah. (Quick speak to God.)

Daily impressed by the poverty of the Indians, Jason decided to show them how to cultivate the soil. By means of a canoe, he made a trip to Fort Vancouver.

Dr. McLoughlin, who had just had his hair trimmed, invited Jason into his living room. While lunch was being prepared, he said: "I've been hearing good reports about your work. The Indians told me that several of their friends have been converted. That's wonderful. He also told me that you've been naming your converts after some of your board members in the East. Let's see—" He patted his hair. "Let's see, I believe one of the girls is Lucy Hedding and one of the boys is Wilbur Fisk. Who are they?" He studied Jason carefully and a curious smile crossed his face.

"Elijah Hedding is the bishop who ordained me and Wilbur Fisk is the one who inspired me to come to the Indians."

McLoughlin laughed. "Are you ever going to name one of them after me?"

"Probably! But we won't give him your name unless he's *really* good-looking—and smart!"

Suddenly McLoughlin became serious. "I'm hoping," he said, "that nothing comes up that could spoil your work."

"What do you mean?"

"When Lewis shot that Blackfoot brave he had no idea of the trouble he was causing. Indians have long memories, extremely long memories. Because of that one dead Blackfoot, the Blackfoot have killed—and scalped!—dozens of whites." He glanced at Jason's thick blond hair.

"Now there is one white man that I want to warn you about."

"What's his name?" asked Jason anxiously.

"Joe Meek! He's as cunning as a snake and as determined as a cannibal with a missionary in his pot. I wouldn't trust him any farther than I could throw him by his nose."

"Do the Indians respect him?"

"That they do. They say he must be made up of ground wild-cat, rattlesnake, and possum all squeezed together. And they're right. We've had a lot of tough mountain men out here. But none is the equal of Joe Meek. And across the years I've known a lot of them. Let's see, I've known Kit Carson, Jim Bridger, 'Brokenhand' Fitzpatrick, 'Cutface' Sublette, and even Old Doc Newell.

"Meek stands over six feet, and is as wicked as Beelzebub himself."

"Why do the Indians respect him?"

"Because he's cunning. He knows when to play possum. And because he's tough. The Indians will never forget the time he met a she-grizzly by himself. Not a night goes by but what that story is relived and even dramatized over an Indian campfire."

"I haven't heard that story," said Jason, fingering his right ear lobe.

"Joe was at the Cross Creeks of Yellowstone when he saw a big she-bear digging roots. That interested him and so he got off his horse and said to a companion, 'Hold her while I kill that b'ar.'

"When he was about forty yards from her, he pulled the trigger. But only the cap went off, and the loud pop scared the bear so much she charged. Poor Old Joe took to his heels. But the bear kept gaining on him. His one hope was that he'd mount his horse and get away.

"But the horse had already taken off. Soon he was at the bottom of the rimrock face-to-face with the bear. And that was a pretty awkward spot to be in. A silvertip can crush a buffalo's skull with one swipe of its paw; and their mouths are crammed with enormous teeth. But even worse than their teeth and fangs is the fact that their vitals are safe behind a boilerplate of fur and at least four inches of fat.

"Somehow Joe managed to get another cap on his gun and jam the barrel into her mouth. But when he pressed the trigger nothing happened. He had forgotten the gun was double-triggered and hadn't been set!

"When the gun finally went off, it was too late; for the bear had knocked it out of his hand and the bullet smacked her in a place that doesn't count."

Jason's jaw sagged and he leaned forward. "What did Joe do then?"

"He was almost scared to death. But he kept his cool. When he thought he was a goner for sure, the bear's two cubs came trotting up. That angered the Old Lady and she boxed the closest one's ears. Joe then had time to get out his knife and try to stab her. But she was too quick. She knocked the knife out of his hand, and it, along with one of his fingers, went sailing into the distance. Then the other cub started nosing around. That really got her dander up. She smacked his ears just like she had smacked the ears of the other one. While she was doing this, Joe managed to jerk his hatchet from off his belt. He aimed at the back of the bear's ear and swung with every bit of strength he possessed. The blade sank into her brain and she fell dead at his feet.

"That daredevil success made Joe Meek a hero. But he does sneaky things. And one of these days the Indians will find him out; and when they do they'll turn on all the whites, including the missionaries!" Deep in thought, McLoughlin paused. Then while lifting an eyebrow, he added "In addition to Joe, there's another man you'd better watch. His name is Peu-Peu-Mox-Mox. We call him Yellow Serpent. He's Chief of the Walla Wallas. Peu-Peu has no love for the whites; and should Joe Meek give him an excuse, bloody massacres may follow."

The conversation was interrupted by the butler. "Table's set," he announced.

During the meal, Jason expressed his plan to plow the acreage around the mission and plant some crops. "We'll show the Indians how to cultivate the land," he explained.

McLoughlin beamed. "You're a man after my own heart," he cried, "and I'll help you. Before you leave I'll supply you with some choice seed."

"How much will it cost?" Jason slanted his eyes at him.

"Nothing. It will be a part of my contribution to your mission."

11

Romance

After amusing and astonishing the Indians by
hitching a horse to a plow, Jason began to cultivate
the thirty acres he had set aside for crops. As the rich
soil curled away from the blade, he felt a surge of joy
which he had not experienced for a long time.

Yes, he, Jason Lee, was introducing a way for the
Indians to provide themselves a living when both the
salmon and the game disappeared!

Having prepared the field, Jason fenced it in order
to keep Indians and cattle and game from tramping
down the crops.

Thoroughly impressed, Dr. McLoughlin lent the
mission seven oxen, a bull and seven cows along with
their calves. This meant that there was now plenty
of milk, and oxen to pull the carts and plow the fields.
Also, it was the beginning of a herd.

As the crops pushed their way through the soil,
Jason decided to develop even more land in the fall;
and again McLoughlin helped. This time he provided
twenty bushels of winter wheat to be used as seed.

During the following winter, Jason dated a letter February 6, 1835, addressed it to the Mission Board, and glowingly noted: "The land here produces good wheat, peas, barley, oats, beans, and potatoes, but Indian corn does not flourish well."

From his correspondence later in the fall, he learned that the name of their mission had been officially changed from The Flathead Mission to the *Oregon* Mission. This was a relief, for he had worried that he would be censured for having located in the Willamette Valley rather than among the Flatheads. But there was another letter that both pleased and puzzled him. This official letter informed him that sometime in July, the ship *Hamilton* would be sailing from Boston in order to bring reinforcements to aid in the work in the Willamette Valley.

That was encouraging. He had pled for new missionaries. And he rejoiced in knowing that among those missionaries were Dr. and Mrs. White. That was great. A physician was desperately needed. Also, his request for young ladies had been fulfilled. But he was disturbed. He fully understood why they were sending Susan Downing, for she was engaged to Cyrus Shepherd. But why, oh why, did they have to send Anna Maria Pittman?

Snorting at the letter, he shoved it over to Shepherd.

The schoolteacher's face was almost radiant as he read it. Then he frowned. "I think the matchmakers are still busy. What are *you* going to do with Anna Maria Pittman?"

Jason all but scowled. "Let me tell you something Cyrus," he rasped, "though a lady should travel the world over to become my wife, yet I could never consent to marry her, unless upon *acquaintance* I should become satisfied that step would be conducive to our mutual happiness—and the glory of God."

Cyrus laughed. "Well, Mr. Lee, I'm glad to see that you've left the door wide open for a possible change of mind," he teased.

Although pleasantly annoyed, Jason could not keep thoughts about Anna Maria Pittman from seeping into his mind. In desperation, he turned his attention to the problem of acquiring a large herd of cattle for both the mission and for that part of Oregon. Oregon, he was convinced, could become a great cattle country.

At that time, only the mission and the Hudson's Bay Company owned cattle, and it was against the trading company's rules to sell even one animal to anyone. Pondering this problem, Jason summoned those who were interested in purchasing cattle to meet at the mission on January 12, 1837.

During this meeting, a joint stock company was organized. Jason put up $400 for the Mission. McLoughlin invested $900 for the Hudson's Bay Company; and Lieutenant William A. Slacum put up another $500. Others invested too, and all together $2700 was raised. At the time, none of the participants realized that this was an historic moment, the beginning of Oregon's great cattle industry.

Slacum, owner of the brig *Loriat,* was immensely pleased. "I will give free passage to California to anyone who wants to buy cattle," he promised.

Convinced that the cattle-buying program was of the Lord, Jason accompanied the buyers to where the Willamette met the Columbia River. There the *Loriat* was gently rocking at anchor and ready. Jason mounted the quarter-deck, motioned the men to gather around him, then lifted his hands and solemnly implored God's blessings on the venture.

Then he disembarked and watched as the ship made its way toward the Columbia, which it would follow to the sea. He hoped that it would not get stuck on

a sandbar before it reached the Pacific and headed
south.

On the way back to the mission, Jason's mind
leaped across the continent to the *Hamilton* which was
supposed to have sailed from Boston on July 28, 1836.
Later, while facing Shepherd across the table, he
said, "It's now February 1837. And that means the
Whites and your beloved, have been on the way for
at least eight months. That's a long time. Do you think
something could have happened to their ship?"

"I-I don't think so. It takes many tedious months
to sail around the Horn and get to Hawaii. And it's
a long way from Hawaii to Oregon."

Jason poured another cup of coffee. "But Cyrus,
ships do go down. Wyeth lost all his goods on his first
ship. And then there are the horse latitudes."

"What are they?"

"Those places where the trade winds stop blowing
and ships can't move for weeks and sometimes even
months."

"But why are they called horse latitudes?"

"Because a ship can only carry so much water; and
when they run out, the first ones to die of thirst are
the horses. Men have had to subsist on a thimbleful
each day." He shuddered.

"You seem terribly worried. Tell me, which
passenger on the *Hamilton* concerns you most?"

"I'm c-concerned about a-all of t-them," Jason
replied with obvious effort.

"Could it be, Superintendent Lee, that you are
especially concerned about a dark-headed young lady
by the name of Anna Maria Pittman?" Cyrus bit his
lip and smiled.

Instead of answering, Jason left the table. But the
crimson flush creeping up his neck and reddening his
cheeks indicated that he was annoyed.

After traveling as far south as San Jose and purchasing eight hundred head of half-wild Spanish cattle, the buyers faced the formidable problem of driving them northward to the Willamette Valley. They faced countless miles of waterless wilderness, mountains, and harsh deserts between them and their destination. The cattle needed both grass and water. And the drivers required a constant supply of kindling to keep warm at night and to cook their food during the day. Often kindling was almost impossible to find.

They camped night after night and continually guarded to keep the cattle from straying or being stolen. "I feel like Moses when he led the Israelites out of Egypt," muttered one of the men after he rounded up a dozen cows that had wandered away.

As months passed, cows died or were killed by wild animals or stolen by Indians. The buyers wearied of their task. "I don't think we'll ever get to Oregon," complained one whose lips were marred with fever blisters.

"Don't give up," replied a tall one who was always reading the Bible. "We'll get there sooner or later. Remember it took Moses forty years to lead the Israelites to the Promised Land. Also keep in mind that it's over twice as far from San Jose to the Willamette Valley as it was from Egypt to the Promised Land."

"Go get lost! You're not much of a comfort," snapped the man with the fever blisters.

But in spite of their losses and the weeks and months of despair, the weary buyers kept plodding toward their destination.

One afternoon while Jason was pacing back and forth worrying about both the cattle and the *Hamilton*, an Indian rapped at his door. "I've just come from

Vancouver," he said, speaking in an Indian language which Jason understood. "Dr. McLoughlin sent me to tell you that the passengers you were expecting from Boston have arrived."

"Wonderful!" exclaimed Jason as he grabbed the messenger's hand. "Tell McLoughlin we'll come immediately." After glancing in the mirror, Jason gave his beard a thorough combing. Then he ordered a pair of Indians from the school to summon the missionaries. While they were gone, he selected his best suit and gave his shoes a fresh polish. He even trimmed his nails.

As soon as the missionaries were prepared, they took their places in canoes and headed downriver on the Willamette. As they, along with their helpers, dipped their paddles, a fresh breeze began to blow against them, slowing their progress a little.

Jason tried to appear at ease, but it was hard for him to hide his anxiety. At Vancouver, McLoughlin gave them a warm greeting and introduced them to the new arrivals. For some reason, he put off introducing Anna Maria to Jason until the very last.

As Jason shook her hand, he noticed that a crimson blush colored her cheeks; and he, himself, was conscious that blood also was rushing up his own neck and reddening his own cheeks.

Thoroughly embarrassed, he tried to hide his feelings. But he was not successful.

On May 25 the newcomers, together with the missionaries accompanied McLoughlin to the wharf. There, they arranged their luggage and took their places in the boat and two canoes that had been prepared for their trip back up the river.

Again, it seemed that some matchmaker was at work; for Jason and Anna Maria were directed to the same canoe.

"Your trip lasted ten months," ventured Jason after they had shoved off. "Were you caught in the horse latitudes?"

"Oh, no. But when we got to Hawaii—and we landed the day before Christmas—we had to wait four months for a ship to bring us here."

"And what did you do in Hawaii?"

"The people—especially the missionaries—were very kind to us. In February we were invited to the wedding of King Kamehameha III. Somehow His Majesty had heard about American wedding cakes; and since he had been told that Susan Downing was a specialist in baking wedding cakes, he asked her to bake one for his wedding; and, I must say, it was delicious." She smiled.

"Did you have any trouble crossing over from Hawaii?"

Anna Maria laughed. "Yes. The *Diana* was supposed to sail on April 5, but we didn't get away until the 8th. Next we stopped at Atooi and took on loads of vegetables. Thus we didn't get *really* started until the 11th. I thought everything would be just right from then on. But I was mistaken. We had three storms that were so bad the sails had to be drawn in. And were we ever sick!'' She shook her head. ''Superintendent Lee, it was terrible.

''I was really glad to see the Oregon coast. But even then the captain was afraid to sail up the Columbia because of the sandbars. So we had to wait two more days for calmer weather—and a high tide.''

''A-are you g-glad you made the trip?'' ventured Jason.

''Of course. God called me to Oregon, and I just know that he has a *special* work for me to do.''

Jason fell into a long silence as he studied her out of the corners of his eyes. Again and again he asked himself, ''Is she the one? And if she is, would she agree to a proposal?''

That evening the boat and canoes dropped anchor near the Pudding River. Two tents were pitched; one for the ladies and one for the men. While the cook prepared coffee and fried thick slices of venison and bear meat over the campfire, a vast array of brilliant stars began to glisten in the sky.

As the pungent aroma of coffee slowly filled the air, Cyrus and Susan kept moving closer and closer on the pine log which they were sharing at the far edge of the glow from the fire.

Jason, who was sitting on the far end of another log on which Anna Maria had parked herself in the center, kept glancing in their direction. Soon the pair were barely a foot apart. Then as the fire burned lower, they began to hold hands. Inspired, Jason turned to Anna and asked, ''How about a little more coffee?''

''Yes, Mr. Lee, I'd like some. This coffee is delicious.''

When Jason returned, he found himself sitting almost a foot closer to Anna Maria than before. Then on the next trip during which he brought her a sizzling slice of bear meat, he deliberately sat even closer. By the time he excused himself to go to bed, he and Anna Maria were considerably less than a yard apart.

Unable to sleep, Jason crept out of his tent and studied the stars. "Oh God," he prayed, "please guide me. Show me what to do, and what to say."

He did not feel any special leadings from the Holy Spirit. When a lonesome coyote began to yap in the distance, it suddenly occurred to him that before he made up his mind, he should find out how Anna reacted to the crude buildings on the mission, and the communal way in which the men were living.

This in mind, he soon fell asleep.

In the morning, they breakfasted on venison and more coffee. While sharing a log with Anna, Jason asked, "Well, Miss Pittman, how did you sleep?"

"I slept very well," she replied. "But Jason," she added after she had swallowed a bite of venison, "we ought to have some bread. Too much meat without any bread isn't good for one."

"True," agreed Jason, flushing a little because she had called him by his first name. "But what can one expect when men do all the cooking? What we need Anna, is a good woman to supervise our meals."

"That's right," she replied with enthusiasm. "Why don't you hire an Indian squaw?"

"Because they don't know how to cook our kind of food," replied Jason. Inwardly, he wondered *is she teasing, fishing, or merely speaking objectively?* Fearing that his face might reveal his thoughts, he asked, "Did you hear that coyote last night?"

"So that's what it was!" she exclaimed.

That evening they arrived at the mission and while Jason was showing the women around, some of the men rearranged the sleeping quarters so that the men could be by themselves. After their brief tour of the farm, Susan Downing said, "I'm going to prepare something to go along with all this meat." She asked an Indian to bring a pail of water and some kindling.

A couple of hours later, the group surrounded a table loaded with fruit, baked potatoes, boiled peas— and a tall stack of pancakes.

The ice broken, Jason and Anna began to share his dreams of a work that would improve the status of all the Indians, regardless of the tribe to which they belonged. In addition they went horseback riding together, exploring the neighboring country.

Again and again Anna expressed enthusiasm about the mission and the work Jason was doing. Then, one evening as the sun began to disappear, he rode up close to her. Working up his courage, he said, "Anna, dear, I think the Lord made us to be one. What do you think?"

"Is this a proposal?" she asked in her matter-of-fact way.

"It is."

"Then I'll have to think about it," she replied as she loosened the reins on the horse and started on her way.

Catching up to her, Jason asked, "When will I have your answer?"

"After I've prayed about it," she replied.

Jason didn't know it, but as she was being outfitted in the East, a member of the board wanted her to take a double mattress with her. But she had been so determined not to marry, she replied, "No, a double mattress is quite unnecessary. Use that extra money for something else."

Jason and Anna continued to ride together; but although they remained on a first-name basis, the subject of marriage was not discussed.

On June 5, however, Anna Maria dispatched a

confidential letter to her parents. "You will be anxious to know," she wrote in her fine and even handwriting, "if there is any prospect of my having a Protector. There is. Mr. Lee has broached the subject, it remains for me to say whether I shall be his helpmate in his important charge. I look unto the Lord who has thus far directed my path. It requires serious deliberation. I know that all eyes will be placed upon me for an example. I am not in haste."

As Jason waited impatiently for her answer, he kept busy directing the missionaries in their work. He was particularly thankful for Dr. and Mrs. White since in recent days a large number of Indians had become seriously ill.

On several occasions he felt an urge to press Anna for an immediate answer. But each time an inner voice seemed to whisper, "Wait." Waiting however, was hard. And this was especially so when he watched the blossoming love between Cyrus and Susan. Nonetheless, he determined to wait.

In the depths of his heart he realized that a mistaken marriage could be utterly tragic—both for him and for the work God had called him to accomplish.

12

The Devil and
Peo-Peo-Mox-Mox

Jason Lee continued to go horseback riding with Anna Maria. But neither from her words nor manner could he determine whether or not she had accepted his proposal. While patiently waiting to find a hint of approval in her black eyes, Cyrus Shepherd approached. "Superintendent Lee," he said, as he struggled to keep a quiver out of his voice, "I-I'd like to have a p-p-private conversation with you."

Lee led him to a pleasant grove of fir trees a short distance from the mission buildings. After they had seated themselves on a log, Jason asked, "What can I do for you?"

"Please, Sir, Susan and I want to set a date for our wedding, a-and we'd l-like for you to perform the ceremony."

"Mmmm. Mmmm," said Jason deep in thought. Then, his face brightening, he added, "I've decided to have our first communion service on Sunday, July 16, at 11 o'clock right here beneath these fir trees. Why don't you and Susan plan to exchange your vows during that service?"

"That would be wonderful," exclaimed Cyrus, getting to his feet.

Jason motioned him back. "But since this will be the *first* Christian wedding in the Northwest, it should be legal and proper."

"What do you mean?" Cyrus asked.

"In that we don't have a government to issue marriage licenses, we must do the next best thing."

"And what is that?"

"The Hudson's Bay Company has a form which we could use. Why don't you go over to Fort Vancouver and get several copies and bring them back?"

"Why several?"

Jason shrugged and a mysterious smile lingered on his face. "You should get several, for your wedding may inspire others to become *legally* married. Some of these whites who are living with squaws ought to change their ways!" He laughed and returned to the mission barn.

While Cyrus was gone to Vancouver, Jason kept hoping that Anna Maria would make up her mind. He even mentioned the forthcoming marriage between Cyrus and Susan to her. Still, she didn't respond. But although she refused to commit herself, she did allow Jason to occasionally hold her hand. And, one night when the moon was particularly bright, she gave his hand an extra squeeze.

This *was* encouraging, even though she wouldn't allow him to give her even a slight peck on the cheek.

As the days meandered by, Jason waited in vain for an answer. Then Cyrus returned from Vancouver. He had the form that should be filled out. Jason studied it eagerly. It read:

Civil Marriage Contract

In the presence of the undersigned witnesses
I............................ a (type of employment)
............................late of (place of birth),
.... and now residing at
.... do voluntarily and on my own
free will and accord take............................
(daughter of)...........................to be my
lawful Wife, and the said ....also
voluntarily and on her free will and accord take
the said Husband .... to be
my lawful Husband.

Witnesses

....
....

Ft. Vancouver
Date
John McLoughlin
C F H B Co.

As Jason studied the form, he imagined how he would fill it out for himself if only Anna would say yes. But, it seemed, that was not to be. Then, following breakfast on Sunday morning, she handed him a carefully folded sheet of paper. "You may want to read that when you are all alone," she said.

"Who wrote it?" he asked

"Read it, and you'll find out," she replied as she walked away.

Unable to wait until everyone left the room, Jason headed for the clump of trees where Cyrus and Susan would be married, and while on the way, he unfolded the sheet of paper. His eyes burned as he read:

Yes, where thou goest I will go,
    With thine my earthly lot be cast;
In pain or pleasure, joy or woe,
    Will I attend thee to the last.

That hour shall find me by thy side,
    And where thy grave is mine shall be;
Death can but for a time divide,
    My firm and faithful heart from thee.

Ruth 1:16,17.   ANNA MARIA

Almost beside himself, Jason laughed. Then he cried. Then he laughed again. "Yes," he assured himself, "Anna Maria Pittman will be mine! And by example we'll show the Indians how to live." As he was rejoicing, he noticed Anna picking flowers in the distance. Rushing over, he sought to embrace her and then kiss her.

"We're not married yet," she replied stepping away.

"Oh, but we will be!"

"True. But until we are, even a kiss is taboo."

Jason laughed. Then he said, "All right, Anna. Just as you say. But let's go for a walk and discuss our wedding plans. Hand in hand, they inched their way over to the clump of elms and sat on a log. There, they planned just where and how they would exchange their vows. At the conclusion, each promised the other that their plans would remain a secret; and that the only one who would know about them would be his nephew, Daniel Lee; and that his lips would also be sealed in regard to the time, the place, the date—and the occasion of their nuptials.

Laughing at their secret, the happy couple squeezed one another's hands and then parted, for the church services were scheduled to start in one hour. He returned to his room to study his notes, while she went to the spring to freshen up.

The next Sunday, July 16, 1837, at 11 a.m. the missionaries, together with a handful of French-Canadians, a number of half-breeds, and about forty Indian children gathered in the open space backgrounded by the clump of fir trees. When all was ready Jason stood in the pulpit and announced the morning hymn.

On their knees, the congregation sang Addison's hymn:

> When all thy mercies, O! my God,
>   My rising soul surveys,
> Transported with the view I'm lost
>   In wonder love and praise.

Then, after they returned to their seats, Jason arose and gave a short exhortation, in the midst of which he said, "I have never advised you to do what is wrong; but on all occasions I have preached that you do what is right. And now I'm going to demonstrate with my own actions that I practice what I preach." He then exchanged the pulpit with Daniel Lee.

Next, as the astonished congregation watched, he boldly stepped out among the people, took Anna Maria by the hand, led her to the front, and stood by her side before his nephew. After answering the questions which Daniel asked as he read from the official Methodist discipline, Jason led his wife back to her seat. While Anna was taking her seat, he realized that she was the first white bride to be legally married in the Northwest.

Then, as the congregation sat transfixed, Jason returned to the pulpit. And Cyrus and Susan came to stand before him. Following their marriage, Charles Roe and his Indian girlfriend also repeated their vows to Jason.

Next, after prayer, Jason preached a sermon based on Numbers 10:29—"Come thou with us, and we will do thee good: for the Lord hath spoken good concerning Israel."

But that wasn't the end of the service!

After the sermon, Jason baptized Charles Roe, and received him into the Methodist Church. Next, Daniel Lee served communion to the fourteen who knelt at the altar. Thus far, the service had been unusually long and many were hoping to be dismissed. But there was an unexpected extension.

Moved by the sight of Roe's baptism, Webley Hauxhurst, a young Quaker from New York, decided that he wanted to be baptized, become a Methodist, and receive communion. After all of this was accomplished, the services were dismissed.

It had been a busy morning!

That October, Jason and Anna were startled by the sound of pounding hoofs and a cloud of dust rising in the distance. As they waited, wondering if this was an Indian attack, they saw a large herd of cattle approaching.

"It's nothing to be worried about," said Jason calmly. "It's the herd of cattle we sent our men to California to buy last January. Let's see. It's taken them about nine months to get here."

Eventually, the cattle were divided. The mission received eight head as their share. "This means that we'll never run short of milk and beef again," remarked Anna. "And it also means that we have started a large cattle business in Oregon," concluded Jason.

Anna Maria was soon appointed housekeeper for the entire mission. Even though she had help, this was a difficult assignment. Nonetheless, she improved the diet of the missionaries along with that of the Indians. Soon all the diners were smelling pumpkin pies, gingerbread, and well leavened bread.

Anna, along with Susan, began to teach the Indian women how to prepare white people's food, how to make soap and how to sew. It was exciting work; and, occasionally, there were things to smile about.

On a Sunday morning a white trader appeared in the services along with his squaw, and baby son. The man's wife, it seems, wanted to follow the ways of the white women. Driven by this ambition, she had secured a little broadcloth; and had made a suit for her baby. The suit was complete with a vest, swallowtail coat and trousers.

The sight of the baby's bare feet sticking out of the tiny trousers was too much for Susan Shepherd. Unable to control her laughter, she became so hysterical she felt compelled to leave. Gaining control, she returned. But just as she sat down Cyrus shook his head at her. That shake sparked another burst of uncontrollable laughter, this one worse than the first.

While the baby's suit was being discussed at the table, Jason asked, "Were his clothes well-made?"

"Oh, yes," replied Susan, nodding her head.

"I think that proves the Indians have great talent," commented Jason rather solemnly. "I've seen some of their carvings, and they're great. It's our Christian duty to help them use their God-given gifts."

Anna wrote to friends in the East about life on the mission: "I have made twelve pounds of butter a week. "We cannot make soap on account of not having fat; and I have been obliged to pay at the Fort 15 cents a pound for fat, vinegar 12 shillings a gallon—the best loaf sugar 15 cents a pound. Some things may be obtained at a moderate price. Money here is of no use. Beaver skins are the money here. They are carried to Vancouver and sold for two dollars twenty cents, and at home would perhaps bring $10. That is why the Traders get rich.''

The newly married couples were supremely happy, and Jason took advantage of their recent marriages to preach a series of sermons on marriage. After he stressed that the New Testament teaches that a man should only have one wife, a newly converted Indian brave confronted him.

''You say that a Christian should only have one wife and that a wife should have only one husband. But is that *really* the truth?'' he demanded.

''Oh, yes,'' replied Jason warmly.

The Indian frowned. ''But Joe Meek teach different.''

''What does he teach?''

''He teach that in the Book of Heaven it say most of the great ones had many wives.''

Jason frowned. ''What were their names?''

''Moses! Abraham! Solomon! David!'' As he named each one, he triumphantly slapped his palm with his finger.

''Ah, but that was long ago,'' explained Jason. ''Those great men lived before the coming of Jesus. In our time a man should have only one wife.''

The Indian shook his head. ''Joe Meek he great man. He killed she-bear with ax, and that is more than any of you missionaries have done. Indians like strong men. We like Joe Meek.'' He patted both cheeks.

''But Joe Meek isn't a Christian. Have you ever heard of Jedediah Smith?''

''Yes, we've all heard of him.''

''Jedediah Smith is a true Christian. He doesn't

drink or smoke. He also fought with a bear. And Jedediah Smith has a Book of Heaven which he reads every day. And Jedediah prays so much he's worn out the knees of his trousers.''

"True. True," replied the Indian as he touched one of the bars of red paint on his check. "But Joe Meek also had a Book of Heaven, and it's a thick one." He indicated the size by making a wide space between his thumb and forefinger.

"I don't know about that," replied Jason. "But I do know that Joe Meek drinks firewater and sells firewater. I've also been told that he's killed Indians.''

The Indian scowled. "I've been thinking about you white missionaries and what you teach. All of you here on the Willamette teach that one can only have one wife. And Marcus Whitman at Waiilatpu and Henry Spalding at Lapwai do the same. Also, you're against slavery. Why?''

"Because one man should not own another.''

"But in the land where you were born they have slaves.'' The Indian grinned in triumph. "We have slaves because we've captured them in battle. Isn't it better to let a man be a slave than to kill him?''

Jason held up his hand. "Come and see me tomorrow," he said.

"I won't come, for I'm getting blankets and some horses in order to buy a new wife." With that he headed for the river and his canoe.

Jason shared the conversation with his wife. "As I was speaking," he added, "I felt as if I were confronting the devil in person." But Anna had an answer: "Jason, God answers prayer! God will take care of Joe Meek. What would you do if Joe became a Christian?''

Jason smiled. "That would be wonderful. And God did change Saul the murderer into Paul the apostle!

It could happen. Joe *does* have a tender place in his heart. Yes, let's be agreed in prayer that God will save Joe Meek.''

There was so much to do, Jason and the other missionaries continued to wish there were eight days in each week. More and more Indians and more and more whites began to attend the services. Concerned about the devastating effect of alcohol among the Indians, Jason founded a temperance society and was pleased to note that many of the white settlers eagerly signed the pledge.

The news of the success of the Oregon Mission spread throughout Methodism. Soon, there were more applicants for missionary work than there was money to send them. In September 1837, new arrivals stepped off the boat and out of their canoes after they made the last portion of their trip up the Willamette. Among these was David Leslie, his wife and two daughters. Also, many farmers began to stream into the country.

It was great to have additional help, but as the number of whites in Oregon increased, so did the concern of the Indians. Night after night they discussed the problem over their campfires. Peo-peo-mox-mox, chief of the Walla Wallas, was especially concerned. While warming his hands at a campfire in the presence of a large number of his braves, he said, ''I'm deeply troubled. First the white missionaries come to teach us from the Book of Heaven, then they begin to farm our land. Next, they invite their friends to come and these friends of theirs also are farming our land.

''This land was given to us by the Great Spirit. It's good land. The Great Spirit has been good to us. He's given us elk, deer, fish. But what will we do when they take all our land? Where will we live? What will

we eat?'' He threw out his hands in a gesture of despair.

The grumblings of Peo-peo-mox-mox and those of other chiefs filtered through to the missionaries, and some of them were frightened.

''Is there any danger that they may attack us?'' asked Anna Maria across the table.

Jason answered, ''Indians have attacked whites before.'' He shuddered. ''If they were to attack us, we'd be helpless. We're not protected by high fences and cannon in the manner of Fort Vancouver.

"But I'm not worried. Our reliance is on the Lord. He has protected us thus far, and he will protect us to the very end."

"That is true," replied Anna in a subdued voice. "But—" She dropped her eyes.

"But what?"

"Jason, I haven't wanted to worry you. Nonetheless, I think you should know that Dr. White has been murmuring against you."

"He has?" Jason's eyes widened.

"Yes, he has; and he's gaining followers."

"His complaint?"

"He says you're not a good organizer."

Jason shrugged. "Maybe he's right." Jason said, reluctantly, "Everyone has a different gift. But don't worry, Anna. The Lord has been inspiring me with some wonderful plans for the work, and He's assured me that He will help us fulfill them." He studied Anna for a long moment. Then after putting his arm around her, he asked, "When's the baby due?"

"Dr. White told me that it will be sometime next June or July."

"Will it be a boy or a girl?" He gave her a tight squeeze.

"I'm sure it will be a boy. At least I hope so." She brushed his cheek with a kiss.

"Why do you want it to be a boy?"

"Oh, that's a secret." She laughed and made a face.

All at once Jason realized that if he followed his plans he would be on his way to the United States when the baby was due. That, of course, would be terrible. Still, God had spoken. Nevertheless, fearing the details would upset Anna, he decided to keep them locked in his heart for at least another few weeks.

13
Trail of Tears

As Jason nervously paced back and forth in front of Anna Maria, he said, "The Lord has given me a difficult assignment. He wants us to establish here a civilization made up of people who are followers of Christ. Oregon could become a Christian community.

"And because I believe I've been ordered by the Lord, I've made a list of the *new* stations we should establish along with the personnel each station will need. Here's the list." He placed it before his wife who was sitting at the table.

"Altogether you will notice that I've listed seven stations. Let's look at two of them.

"At *Umpqua* we'll need a missionary, a farmer, and a doctor. And at *Nesqually* we'll need a missionary and a farmer. What do you think of that?"

"How many missionaries will you need to manage all those seven stations?"

"A minimum of twenty-five."

"Twenty-five! And h-how will they be supported?" Anna bit her lip.

Jason laughed. "God owns the cattle on a thousand hills; all the salmon in the Columbia, and all the buffalo on the plains."

"And how will you persuade the Board to agree with you. They'll just file your letter and forget it."

"Ah, now you've opened the sore spot. Anna, dear, I don't intend to write to them. I will go and see them in person."

"In person! A-and l-leave me a-alone? What about the baby?" Her jaw dropped open.

"Doctor White will be here. He'll deliver it, and Leslie, my assistant, will take care of all the business matters."

"But what about Peo-Peo-Mox-Mox? When he learns that you're gone he may burn the mission and—kill all of us. Would you like that to be on your conscience?" She wiped her eyes.

"Anna Maria, remember we must rely on the Lord."

Choked with emotion, Anna sobbed out loud and blew her nose.

"Don't cry," comforted Jason. "I shall leave the decision up to you. If you say no, I won't go. But I do hope you'll agree because if I go in person, I can speak in a lot of churches on the way, raise money and persuade dozens of Methodists to move out here and help civilize the country. Just think, Anna, if hundreds of good, honest people moved here, it wouldn't be long until most of the population would be American; and then it would only be a short time until Old Glory would be snapping in the breeze."

"I'll have to pray about it," replied Anna, forcing a smile.

Three days later, Anna Maria said, "I've prayed through and the good Lord has helped me make a decision, hard though it is."

Suddenly her eyes began to overflow. Then, as she wiped her tears she handed Jason a folded sheet of paper.

Jason smiled and eagerly unfolded the little note. Then he, too, began to weep, for he knew the words came from the very depths of her heart. Splashed with tear marks, Anna's poem was heartbreaking. It read:

> Farewell husband, while you leave me,
>   Tears of sorrow oft will flow;
> Day and night will I pray for thee,
>   While through dangers you may go:
> Oh, remember,
>   Her who loves you much: Adieu.

Jason held out his arms and as they clung together, he murmured, "It will be at least a year and a half before I see you again. But remember we'll both be having instant communion with one another through Christ." As he released her, he accidently knocked over a glass of milk.

Dashing for the mop, Anna, laughed through her tears. Then she threw her arms around Jason and murmured, "You're just as clumsy as ever. But since the Lord has supplied us with more cows I guess it's all right."

Both of them laughed, and he kissed her again.

On the morning of March 26, Jason, along with Philip Edwards, and two Indian boys, stepped gingerly into a canoe and headed for Vancouver. Anna Maria watched until they were out of sight, and then she climbed the steps, threw herself across the bed and wept. It was indeed terrible to be alone!

As she wept, she suddenly realized that it was time to prepare dinner. She put some shavings, a bit of paper, and more firewood into the stove, and blew the coals into a flame. Then she selected a choice piece of venison roast, several vegetables, and slowly began to prepare them. While peeling the potatoes, cutting the tops from the onions, and trimming the carrots, it occurred to her that this would be Jason's favorite dinner. That thought inspired a fresh deluge of tears.

Eventually she gained control and rang the dinner-bell; but when only three sat at the table, her eyes overflowed again. Two days later, she received a letter from Jason. It had obviously been written while he was on the way to Vancouver. That letter was like meat and drink. She reread it many times.

Knowing he would be in Vancouver for several days, Anna responded immediately. She entrusted the letter to a trader who was on his way to the Fort for supplies.

In her second letter which she addressed to the place where she thought he'd be stopping, she mentioned that since Dr. White was a little concerned that she might miscarry, he had sentenced her to bed. This was bad news, and she knew it would worry Jason. Still, she felt that he should know the truth. Jason had always been honest with her and she was determined to continue to be honest with him, even though her honesty was painful.

By forcing herself, Anna remained in bed days at a time. The Bible, especially the psalms, became a special comfort; and each day she spent several hours in prayer. "O, Lord," she kept repeating as she knelt by the side of her bed, "watch over Jason, and may his dreams for a new Oregon come to pass."

Each day she hoped for a letter from him, but since there was no regular mail service, she was usually disappointed. Then on April 14, she received a package. That package contained his watch, along with two letters. She read and reread them until they became a part of the tissue of her life. Then she began to imagine where he might be. *It's now 10 o'clock, Friday morning. What is he doing? Is he well? Are the Blackfoot after him? Are his clothes holding out? Have any of his buttons dropped off? Does he have enough thread? Is it the right color? Is he getting enough to eat?*

Jason, too, was equally concerned about Anna Maria; and all during the day, he found himself praying for her safety. On April 18, Jason and his companions arrived at the Lapwai Mission near what is now Lewiston, Idaho. There, he was a guest of Henry and Eliza Spalding, Presbyterian missionaries who had arrived in late November, 1836.

As the Spaldings showed Jason around the house they were building, Mrs. Spalding burst out, "I can't wait until it's finished. When we first came, we had to live in a lodge made of buffalo skins. The lodge was only fifteen feet in diameter. But, in spite of that, we used thirty buffalo hides."

"It was cold that winter," put in Eliza. "Even so, we were fairly warm."

During the week, the Spaldings provided shelter for Jason and his party. In the middle of a conversation over a campfire, the name of Joe Meek came up. "And what do you know about him?" asked Jason. "I understand that he's teaching that one can be a Christian and have more than one wife."

"I'm afraid that's the truth," replied Spalding as he pushed a log deeper into the fire. "Joe Meek is a first class soundrel. This is what happened:

"One day he arrived at Chief Kowesote's camp. He's one of our Nez Perce converts. Meek was loaded with beaver skins. But he didn't want to sell any of them. The scoundrel had only one thing in mind: He wanted to buy a wife! And he already had one in mind. He wanted to marry the younger sister of Doc Newell's wife.

"Now Joe knows all the tricks to deceive the Indians, and since he was admired for having killed that old she-bear with an ax, he knew that he could get the Indians to do just about anything he wanted them to do. The Nez Perce think he's almost a god."

Spalding pushed the log deeper into the fire. "When Joe first arrived at the camp, he found that the chief and his braves wanted to hear about the Book of Heaven, and he told them that he was a preacher. Somewhere he borrowed a Bible and preached a few sermons. At the end of his stay, Kowesote asked him what he would like for his pay, and do you know what the scoundrel said?"

"What?"

Spalding was silent for a moment as he thoughtfully stroked his long beard. "Meek said, 'I want to marry the younger sister of Doc Newell's wife.'

" 'Oh, but you already have a wife; and Spalding and Whitman have taught us that a Christian can only have one wife. Indeed, they've made some of us give up our extra wives!' exclaimed Kowesote.

"To that, this snake-in-the-grass replied, 'The Book of Heaven don't teach no such thing. Come tonight and I'll show you what it really teaches.' He then read to them about Abraham and Solomon and David and a few others."

"And so?"

"And so he married Doc Newell's sister-in-law. Ah, but that wasn't the end. Oh, no. Joe also pulled another shenanigan."

"What did he do?"

"After Kowesote gave him one of his daughters, Meek demanded that he be compensated with extra pay for all of his sermons. I've been told by a witness that Joe left the camp with thirteen horses, a pile of first class beaver skins, a buffalo robe and a few other things."

"What can we do with Joe Meek?" asked Jason.

"I-I don't know." Spalding shrugged. "Since we have no government we have no law."

"We can pray," cut in Eliza, nodding her head with conviction. "God took care of Ananias and Sapphira, and he can take care of Joe Meek!"

From Lapwai, Jason and his party continued on toward St. Louis. He joined an American Fur caravan, so his trip was now much easier.

As spring approached, life became exceedingly lonely for Anna Maria. Day after day she hoped that she would have a letter from Jason. But she realized that this was an impossibility unless he met someone headed for Vancouver. She tried to keep busy, but each day was dogged by her nagging illness.

Indian mothers who had children came to the mission and tried to comfort her. Still, it was hard for her to keep a cheerful attitude.

On Thursday morning, June 21, Anna Maria summoned Dr. White. Two days later she gave birth to a son. But on the following Monday, the baby died; and the next morning she, too, passed away. Her last words were: "I am going to my rest."

David Leslie preached the funeral sermon. With the baby in her arms, she was buried in a wooden casket near the spot by the clump of fir trees where she had exchanged vows with Jason only a year before. The casket was built by the mission carpenter. The next problem was to contact Jason.

From Vancouver an express messenger was rushed to Lapwai. There, knowing that a carrier would have to go through dangerous Blackfoot country, Henry Spalding hired six Indian braves to transport the bundle of letters to Fort Hall.

It required sixteen days to reach the Fort. After

some searching, a Mr. Richardson, accompanied by E.G. Curtis, were selected to continue eastward with the precious package. While crossing the Rockies, the two were surrounded by Indians. Attempting to make them prisoners, the Indians seized the bridles of their horses. Miraculously, the carriers escaped, but the Indians captured their packhorses and rode away with them. The packhorses were loaded with all their vital provisions.

Without food, and afraid to shoot any of the abundant game for fear of attracting Indians, Curtis and Richardson jogged along on their mounts without a bite of food for five days.

Finally, after more than two months of relentlessly pushing eastward, the two haggard men reached the house where Jason was staying at Westport, just west of the Missouri frontier.

Although it was one o'clock in the morning, they pounded at the door until Jason appeared.

"We have bad news for you," said E.G. Curtis as he handed him the bundle. Jason stumbled over to a chair, lit some candles, and ripped open the package. Soon he was weeping. "Anna Maria is gone," he wailed. "And so is my son. I'm now a widower! What, oh, what will I do? Yes, what will I ever do?"

"Would you like to return to Oregon with us?" ventured Richardson.

"I-I d-don't know. Let me pray about it. I'll give you my decision in the morning." He then found a place for them to sleep and arranged for the care of their horses.

He rolled and tossed and kept readjusting his pillow, or he paced the floor. He also prayed, and wept, and thought. The question that churned in his mind was: *Should he return to Oregon, or should he continue on?* Being a practical man, he realized that even if he returned to Oregon he could do nothing about the situation. Anna Maria and his son were dead. Moreover, they had gone to be with the Lord. He remembered the last two lines of the poem Anna had prepared in response to his proposal.

Getting up, he studied the stars. Then as he thought of eternity, he quoted those, now almost sacred, lines to himself:

> Death can but for a time divide
> My firm and faithful heart from thee.

Comforted, he fell asleep. Then, awakened by the loud crowing of a rooster, he knelt by the side of his bed. He prayed about the places where he wanted to establish satellite missions, and the names paraded before his eyes: *Umpqua, Sandimans Fork, Willamette Falls, Nesqually, Cowelits, Wascopan . . . .*

He remembered how Jesus replied to a disciple who wanted to delay his commitment by taking time to bury his father. Jesus' blunt answer, 'Follow me; and let the dead bury their dead' (Matt. 8:22) burned like a glowing ember in his heart. *Yes, that was God's message. He would continue on to New York, present his plans to the Board, and inspire them to appoint additional missionaries.* Also, he would speak in churches across the land and inspire followers of Christ to migrate to Oregon.

He dressed and announced to his visitors that God had given him a mission, and that he would continue on to New York City.

''You're a dedicated man,'' commented Richardson at the breakfast table.

Jason smiled. ''I try to be.''

Jason, together with the Indian lads he had brought, continued to journey eastward by canoe on the Missouri River. Everywhere Jason stopped, doors were flung wide open. The lure of Indian converts, especially flat-headed "Indian Tom," crowded each building; and Jason's messages inspired listeners both to offer their services as missionaries and to sell out and move to Oregon.

Pressing eastward, they stopped at the village of Chicago. Then, by means of the Great Lakes, they continued on toward New York City. They reached their destination on the last day of October.

The Board was profoundly impressed and was inspired to approve most of Jason's plans. "But we'll need lots of money," said a money-conscious spokesman. "How about remaining in New England until the money is raised?"

Jason's tight itinerary booked him to speak at a different place almost every night. People were generous with their money. And tired though he was, God rewarded him with the needed strength to continue the nerve-shattering schedule. Newspapers were supportive. And frequently the mayor of a city was on the platform.

One Sunday evening Jason stood behind the pulpit of the First Congregational Church in Montpelier, Vermont. As he studied the audience, he became aware of a striking young lady in the congregation. He could not keep from glancing in her direction; and every time he did so, he noticed that she was completely taken up with his message.

After the service, he approached the pastor as he was clearing papers from the pulpit. Somewhat nervously, he asked, "Who is that young lady who sat near the front on the right hand side and who seemed so interested in our work in Oregon?"

"Oh, that's Lucy Thomson. She was just graduated as valedictorian at the Newberry Seminary. Quite an achievement. They have an enrollment of 326. Great school. Missionary in spirit."

"Mmmm. And where was she born?" Jason fingered the lobe of his ear.

"In Barre, Vermont."

"Mmmm. Mmmm. That's interesting. Barre is only a little over forty miles from Stanstead, Lower Canada, where I was born."

"Would you like to meet her?"

"Oh, no. I'm too busy to be visiting young ladies." He hesitated. Then, screwing up his courage, he asked, "B-but i-is she s-single?" Jason studied the pastor's face carefully.

"As far as I know she is."

A little flustered, Jason accidentally knocked a pot of gardenias onto the floor with his elbow. Fortunately, the pot didn't break. "Oh, no, I'm sorry," he apologized.

"That's quite all right, Superintendent Lee," replied the pastor as he gently knelt and replaced the flowers into the pot. "You were a great blessing to all of us. God has given you a remarkable gift of communication."

As the pastor turned to leave, a mysterious smile brightened his face.

14
Heartbreak

After a brief stop at Stanstead, Jason continued his tour. Hopeful young ladies came early in order to get front seats. But none of them, fancy hats or not, were as attractive as Lucy.

Tormented by memories of her, he finally sent her a brief matter-of-fact letter. Lucy responded immediately.

Soon Jason and Lucy were facing one another across a table. Then they began exchanging letters regularly. Next they took slow walks in the moonlight. Jason knew he was falling in love. But he was concerned. Would it create a scandal for him to marry even before he had visited Anna Maria's grave? As he pondered, he decided to counsel with leaders of the Missionary Board.

"How long has it been since the death of Anna Maria?" asked a triple-chinned member as he studied Jason through his pince-nez.

"Over a year," replied Jason.

"Then there is no reason why you shouldn't

remarry. And take it from me, Lucy is a fine young lady.''

Jason and Lucy were married in the Methodist Church in Barre, Vermont, on July 28, 1839. Following a short honeymoon and more lectures, the happy couple prepared to sail to Oregon on the *Lausanne*, by way of Cape Horn. It was wonderful not to become saddle sore. But Jason was concerned.

While watching a school of flying fish from a deck chair next to Lucy's, Jason reached for her hand. ''I think we'd better start praying about the future of our work in Oregon,'' he murmured. He spoke softly for fear of being overheard.

''What do you mean?'' she asked.

''I was hoping for about twenty-five workers. But the Board has sent a lot more. Including Indian Tom, there are fifty-one would-be-missionaries on this ship!'' He shook his head.

''Why should this be upsetting?'' Lucy smiled and pointed at a nearby whale that was spouting water.

''Because we're not ready for that many workers. It takes time to find one's place in the body of Christ. Did you know that we have six preachers on board?'' He shuddered.

''But aren't the fields 'white already to harvest'?''

''They are. But with too many preachers swinging scythes in the same field, someone is going to lose his head. Lucy, one of the worst things we have to contend with is the green-eyed monster. The problem is: far too many people want to be king of the hill. The apostles were saintly men, but the Holy Spirit guided them into separate parts of the world.''

''Oregon is a big field.'' Lucy slanted her eyes at him.

''True. Nonetheless, there must be a single leader. 'If a house be divided against itself, that house cannot

stand' (Mark 3:25). Ah, but let's not worry. God will
see us through.''

After a voyage of nearly eight months, they sailed
into the mouth of the Columbia. But, due to the
sandbars, another two weeks were required to reach
Fort Vancouver. As they awaited high tides so they
could skim over the sandbars, Jason stood with Lucy
at the rail. ''We'll soon be at our place of service,''
he said. ''The romance of our trip is nearly over. The
hard part is just ahead. In a few days we'll be
contending with Peo-peo-mox-mox, Joe Meek, the
beast with the green eyes and a missionary board that
is three thousand miles away and is subject to any
rumor that drifts to their doors. Soon, as
superintendent, I'll have the duty of assigning each
missionary to a certain field and a certain
occupation.'' He sighed. ''Some of them will be
unhappy. Be sure and say an extra prayer for me.''

When they reached Fort Vancouver, Dr.
McLoughlin was again a welcome host. He provided,
food, rooms and a place where Jason could meet with
the missionaries and announce their duties.

Although there was grumbling, the missionaries
complied with his directives. After the last one
embarked on his assignment, Jason blew a sigh of
relief. Nonetheless, he was worried. Confiding to
Lucy, he said, ''I hope we don't have mutiny. But
I can almost smell one coming.'' He buried his face
in his palms and shuddered.

Within hours after his return, Jason discovered that
Dr. White had overdrawn his account at Fort
Vancouver and had also, without authorization,
drawn heavily on the mission account.

Ten days after Jason's return, White brought him
a record of his accounts. ''There, Mr. Lee, you can
see that I drew money from the mission account in

order to build a hospital.''

Jason glanced at the figures. His only reply was a soft ''Mmmm. Mmmm.''

''Why don't you write *settled* across each page?'' asked White.

''But I can't do that until I've studied them!'' exclaimed Jason.

The doctor stared. ''Do you m-mean that you don't believe me?'' he demanded.

''I didn't say that. But as superintendent, it's part of my job to make sure the accounts are accurate. It's easy to make a slip.''

White's face darkened. ''I don't relish being mistrusted,'' he snapped as he strode out of the room.

Jason was disturbed. From the beginning of Elijah White's assignment, a dark cloud had hovered above his life. Nathan Bangs had been told that the doctor had skipped numerous unpaid debts at the time of his departure for the Northwest. Also, many in Oregon felt that he was too familiar with some of the missionary ladies.

Trouble continued to brew between Superintendent Lee and Doctor White, and often as Jason and Lucy sat at the table they noticed that little cliques were developing. Sometimes they became aware of body communication—lifted eyebrows, nodding heads, the meeting of eyes—between White's followers.

Finally, after four months of simmering on a low fire, the animosity among the missionaries began to smoke and bubble. Then, four months after it had started, Alvin Waller arranged for a group to investigate the charges against White. The result of this ''jury'' made up of White's peers was that he was dismissed.

Losing control, White threatened Jason that he would either ride him out on a rail or see him shamed before the Board.

White and his family returned to the United States on board the *Lausanne*, the same ship that had brought the reinforcements.

Jason and Lucy were heartsick.

The Lees worked night and day to reach both Indians and whites, and hundreds of families continued to stream over the Oregon Trail into the land Jason had described as bursting with possibilities. This huge influx of pioneers, increased the problems: What would Peo-peo-mox-mox do? Would there be bloody massacres? And where would pioneer children attend school?

Along with these concerns, Jason worried about completing the move of the mission from its original location to Chemeketa about ten miles south of what is now Salem. The new location, he was convinced, was a much better one. Bordered on the east by a forest and on the west by the Chemeketa plains, it was an ideal spot. A little stream known as Mill Creek flowed across the property. This stream, he believed, was just what was needed to operate a grist mill that could earn its way by supplying flour. Indeed, he felt assured that there was sufficient water to also operate a sawmill. Thoroughly inspired, he got busy.

On January 17, 1842, a group that was interested in establishing a school met in Lee's new parsonage. Jason was elected chairman. Soon money began to come in. By-laws were adopted, publicity was sent out—and a building was erected. The school was named *Oregon Institute*.

Amidst this activity, Jason was so busy he almost forgot that he was scheduled to become a father in February. Then on the 28th of that month, Lucy presented him with a fine, healthy daughter.

"And what shall we name her?" he asked.

"I-I don't know," replied the new mother. "If it

had been a boy I would have suggested Jason."

"Then her name is Lucy," replied Jason with enthusiasm.

"But what about a middle name?" asked Lucy. She bit her lip as she pondered. Then she said, "I know, I know what it should be. It should be Anna Maria!"

"Oh, but that was my first wife's name," replied Jason.

"True. But your first wife should be remembered."

Jason glowed. "Then her name is Lucy Anna Maria," he replied with obvious satisfaction.

Jason was supremely happy. Lucy Anna Maria became a showpiece. As friends rocked her in their arms, he often proudly asked, "Well, what do you think of our little missionary?"

Less than three weeks later, the mother became seriously ill. Lingering by her side, Jason did all he could. But he was helpless. On the 20th of March, while Jason was holding her hand, she gasped once or twice, and was gone.

While cuddling the baby in his arms, Jason watched as his wife and the mother of his daughter was lowered into the grave that had been dug next to that of his first wife.

As he walked away, he remembered again that this little cemetery backgrounded by trees was the scene of his first marriage. Lucy's death meant that he had lost two wives and a son in less than five years. He was overwhelmed. But within hours he took refuge in Paul's statement: "And we know that all things work together for good to them that love God, to them who are the called according to his purpose" (Romans 8:28).

Jason didn't have time to linger with grief. He was far too busy. He had to arrange for someone to take care of Lucy Anna Maria; and he also kept hearing alarming reports about unrest among the Indians.

"Peo-peo-mox-mox is preparing for war, " said a recent Indian convert.

"The Indians are buying guns and sharpening their tomahawks," reported another.

Jason tried to patiently wait for the Indians to calm down. But they did not calm down. The arrival of every new pioneer increased the volume and length of their war dances.

Then, when Doctor Elijah White returned to Oregon in the fall of 1842 with a long immigrant train, the fury of the Indians began to overheat. They were especially angry because they learned that White had been commissioned by the Federal Government in Washington.

One morning an Indian Christian approached. "Superintendent Lee," he said, "in a recent powwow some of the braves of Peo-peo-mox-mox began to talk about attacking the Wascopam mission. They are foaming with anger. They say the palefaces want to steal their hunting grounds."

"What should I do?" asked Jason.

"Maybe if you would go and see Peo-peo-mox-mox you could persuade him to calm his men. If you don't, every paleface at Wascopam will be killed."

"Go back and tell Peo-peo-mox-mox that I will come to Wascopam and have a discussion with him during the first week of February. Tell him that I am his friend," replied Jason promptly.

When some of the missionaries learned about Jason's plans, they were alarmed. "Yellow Serpent is a very powerful man," said one. "He would kill you with as little thought as a Chinook fisherman would spear a salmon."

Ignoring the warnings he heard from both Indians and missionaries, Jason secured a Chinook canoe, and employed four Indians to guide and row the canoe. Equipped with only a tent, a few blankets, and some kettles in which to prepare food, he set out downstream on the Willamette.

The date was January 3, 1843.

It was cold, and the river was swollen from recent rains. At Fort Vancouver, they entered the Columbia and headed east toward the Wascopam mission near The Dalles, the place where he had arranged for Peo-peo-mox-mox to meet him.

The Columbia was cold and there were chunks of ice bobbing around them. Moreover, they had to paddle upstream. Also, there was a heavy snow, and frequent storms of sleet. As they slowly made their way up the river, Jason kept praying that God would give him wisdom and soften Yellow Serpent's heart.

Jason found the missionaries at Wascopam modestly concerned about their possible fate. But, on the whole, they were cheerful. Daniel Lee, along with his wife and two children, were part of the group.

While there, Jason served communion, preached several times and was a most welcome visitor.

Eventually, the dreaded day of crisis came. A messenger alerted the missionaries that Peo-peo-mox-mox had arrived and was prepared to counsel with Jason.

"I think I had better go and see him by myself," said Jason. "But first, let's pray that God will inspire me to say just the right thing."

As he headed toward the appointed place, Jason felt an unusual confidence. But when he got there, and noticed that Yellow Serpent was surrounded by braves with slashes of paint on their cheeks, he had a moment of intense insecurity. Although, like himself, they were *apparently* unarmed, he remembered that the Indians who massacred the crew of the *Tonquin* were also *apparently* unarmed when they stepped on deck.

Forcing a smile, Jason stepped forward and held out his hand. Peo-peo-mox-mox responded, but there was no warmth in his greeting. As he stood before the chief of the Walla Wallas, Jason noticed his Oriental eyes, his long black hair which was parted beneath his hat and streamed like frayed rope down his shoulders. He also noticed his high cheek bones, triangular nose, and firm chin.

"It is indeed a pleasure to meet you," said Jason, "and I've heard that you've traveled one hundred miles to be here."

"True," responded Yellow Serpent. "We've come a long way because our hearts are heavy. And we've come to you because the reports are that you love the Indians."

"Thank you," replied Jason. "Now tell me what's on your heart."

"When you first came there were very few palefaces in our land. Now our country is full of them. Soon, there will be more and then more and then more. Before your friends came we had plenty of game. Now there is not so much because your people kill animals for sport with their guns. We, with our bows and arrows, only kill enough for our necessities. Speak, White Man, and answer my questions. How long will we be able to continue living in this land which the Great Spirit was pleased to give us? Are the whites always going to be rich and the Indians remain poor?"

"That will depend largely on yourselves," replied Jason. "If you imitate our industry and adopt our habits your poverty will disappear. Our hands are our wealth, and you and your people have hands as well as we."

Yellow Serpent then had another question: "Does

Doctor White, the official from your government in Washington, intend to give us presents?''

Jason's reply was as diplomatic as he could make it. But he was frank to say that industrious people would rather labor for a thing than to beg for it.

After more conversation, Jason parted from the Indians hoping that he had created an atmosphere of goodwill, but the frowns on the faces of Yellow Serpent and his braves indicated that they were far from satisfied.

Back at Wascopam, Jason was optimistic in his report to the missionaries. ''My advice,'' he said, ''is that you be extremely careful in your dealings with the Indians. Don't provoke them in any way. Show by example that they can acquire wealth in horses and cattle by means of farming and thrift.''

To this, Henry Brewer, the missionary farmer, replied, ''I'm doing my best, and I am getting some response. In time, they'll begin to learn this.''

''I'm sure they will,'' encouraged Jason. ''When I was at Lapwai, Henry Spalding told me that an Indian walked three hundred miles in order to get potatoes for planting. That's progress.

''One more thing. We're planning a camp meeting this summer. If we could get a *real* revival started, it would solve a lot of problems. Keep announcing it, and keep praying that God will have his way.''

As Jason turned to leave, Daniel approached. ''Uncle Jason,'' he said, ''my wife and I have decided to return to the United States. We've been here nearly ten years, and that's enough for us.''

Jason tried to change his mind. Unable to do so, he headed toward the canoe with an expanding lump in his throat.

15

Pointed Fingers

Jason grieved over the loss of his nephew and his wife. Daniel and Sarah had been a great help; moreover, he had been able to confide his troubles to them. But now that they were gone, he quenched his grief by concentrating on the summer camp meeting he was planning. Since this would be the first camp meeting aimed at whites ever conducted in Oregon, he determined it would be so effective that other camp meetings could be planned.

Camp meetings had been promoted by Bishop Asbury; and they were all the rage in Methodism. Often, one thousand such meetings were conducted in a single summer.

An excellent location was selected about thirty-five miles west of Willamette Falls. Special advertising was sent by carriers to all the whites in the area. The bulletin announced that the meeting would open on July 13. And since Jason hoped that members of all denominations would attend, he arranged for Harvey Clark, a Congregational minister, to be in charge.

Jason also selected a fine battery of ministers to be the speakers. This group, along with himself, included H.K.W. Perkins and Gustavus Hines.

As Jason was setting up his tent under the shade of a magnificent oak and a pair of extremely tall elms, he remarked, ''I do hope that at least some of these unsaved pioneers will give their hearts to the Lord. Oregon should become a Christian state; and that's even more important than for it to be a part of the Union.''

After the seats were put in place and the tables arranged where the visitors could dine, the missionaries waited anxiously for the first service. Each hoped every seat would be taken.

But when the first service began on Thursday evening, only fourteen Indians straggled in. Not a single visiting white appeared. Masking his disappointment, Jason preached on Matthew 18:20—''For where two or three are gathered together in my name, there am I in the midst of them.''

The next night, however, the attendance increased; and by Sunday it skyrocketed to 60. Nineteen of the pioneer whites present were not professing Christians. Inspired like a pig in a cornfield, the preachers were at their best.

Sixteen of the nineteen were converted. One of the whites there was the notorious mountain man, Joe Meek. Joe got to his feet, and all eyes were upon him. One thought tensed every face. The entire audience leaned forward, wondering what this concentration of evil who'd lost a finger during his fight with a she-bear would do. As they viewed his stolid, grimy face, they remembered that he had pretended he was a preacher. Several sought reassurance by touching their holsters.

Their concern was groundless. In a clear but husky

voice, Joe Meek said: "Tell everyone you see that Joe Meek, that old Rocky Mountain sinner, has turned to the Lord."

That evening in private, when someone asked Jason about the genuineness of Meek's conversion, he replied, "From the moment I learned that Joe had wept when his cronies began to play cards on a dead man's back, I knew that Joe had a tender place in his heart. Also, I've been praying for him for many years.

"But we'll wait and see if he can prove his conversion by bearing a little fruit."

The missionaries didn't have to wait long. Meek had one of them marry him to the Indian girl with whom he was living. He was baptized and had his now-legal wife baptized, and changed her name to Virginia in honor of the state where he was born.

1843 was a pivotal year in the history of Oregon.

Without people noticing it, a legal government had slowly been evolving. When Ewing Young died without a will in 1841, the pioneers wondered what they should do with his property.

Jason had a suggestion: "Let's elect a judge to take care of Young's estate."

Since Jason had already introduced democracy when he founded the Oregon Temperance Society, his idea pleased the pioneers, so they met and elected Methodist missionary, Doctor Ira Babcock, judge. This move was so successful it was decided that when they had another major problem they would assemble and vote in another solution. The next problem faced them sooner than expected.

The new problem concerned wolves, panthers, bears and other predators that were killing their horses and other livestock. Seeking a solution, they announced a "wolf meeting." At this meeting they decided to pay cash for the skins of any predators that were delivered to an elected official.

Again, their solution turned out well. Inspired, they called another "wolf meeting." At this meeting a committee was appointed to create plans for a government.

The new committee announced a meeting to be held at Champoeg on May 2, 1843. At the beginning of the meeting, the first reaction was almost completely negative. Then Joe Meek leaped to his feet. After drawing a line in the dirt, he shouted "Who's for a divide? All for the report of the committee and organization follow me." Most of the Americans and two of the French-Canadians followed Meek. The others left the meeting. At the conclusion, those remaining decided to meet again at Champoeg two months later.

At this second meeting a provisional government was formed. The word "provisional" meant that it would remain in power until a boundary line could be settled.

The structure of this government was simple. Instead of a governor, the country would be "managed" by an executive committee of three. All laws would be enacted by a "legislative committee" of nine. Slavery was prohibited. But free Negroes were barred. Also, there would be no taxes. Instead of taxes, the expense of government would be met by "donations." In addition, at Jason Lee's suggestion, each adult male could claim a square mile of land. But in order to claim this land he had to describe his claim and register it at the recorder's office.

This constitution didn't last. Following a new wave of settlers which outnumbered the previous pioneers, the "executive committee" was replaced with a governor.

The first governor was another Methodist missionary, Doctor George Abernathy.

Also, it was decided that the government should be supported by taxes. Moreover, Joe Meek was elected sheriff; and his major duty was to collect taxes!

Feeling the need of more democracy, the legislative committee was increased from nine to thirteen members. Also five counties: Clatsop, Clackamas, Champoeg, Yamhill and Tualatin were formed. And, to the dismay of some, Vancouver County, just north of the Columbia, was added to the previous five counties. Including Vancouver County was controversial because some of its land was controlled by the Hudson's Bay Company.

Jason was excited about the "Oregon fever" that was gripping the United States. Nonetheless he was worried. Cliques among the missionaries were solidifying. He also noticed an increasing hardening of glances when he was present.

This "body language," together with the fact that his letters from the Board had not been as enthusiastic as they had been before 1840, caused him to wonder. In addition, his suspicions deepened when he noticed the thick envelopes several of the missionaries were sending, and *receiving* from the Board.

Eventually, it occurred to him that Doctor White, along with W.W. Kone, and Doctor Richmond, men with whom he differed, were in the East; and were, undoubtedly, at that very moment, turning the Board against him. And this he knew was an easy task, for none of the Board had ever been in the Northwest. What was he to do?

After days of prayer and searching the Bible, he decided he would return to the United States and speak to the Board face-to-face. That was a difficult decision, for he didn't want to leave his work which was showing signs of remarkable growth.

Jason and Lucy Anna Maria, who was now almost two, together with Gustavus Hines and his wife, booked passage for Hawaii on the *Columbia*. They climbed the gangplank on Christmas Day, expecting to sail immediately. But when the anchor was not lifted for more than a week, Jason approached the captain.

"We're facing a southeast wind," replied the plump, ruddy-faced man with a smile. "And that's almost opposite what it should be. Also, we must have high tide so that we can cross the sandbars."

Eventually, the captain ordered the sails hoisted and the ship was on its way. As Jason stood with little Lucy Anna Maria in his arms and watched the Oregon coast gradually fade out of sight, he had to contend with a rush of tears.

Because of several storms, it took three and a half weeks to reach Oahu and finally drop anchor in Honolulu Bay. "Well, this part of our trip is over," exulted Jason as he held Lucy up for a better view.

His face laced with confidence and smiles, Jason stepped ashore. But his joy didn't last. "You are no longer the superintendent," said the local Methodist pastor as he helped load his things into a wagon.

"What do you mean?" demanded Jason, standing still and staring.

"You've been replaced by Reverend George Gary of the Black River Conference in New York."

"I-I've b-b-b-been r-r-replaced?" stammered Jason.

"Gary is on his way now. He's coming by the way of the Horn. He'll be in Oregon in a couple of months or so."

"But, I can h-h-hardly believe it." Jason's jaw sagged, and he gripped the pastor's shoulder to keep from falling.

The pastor said kindly, "You should have been notified. Perhaps your letter from the Board is in Oregon."

Jason pulled himself together. He arranged a conference that afternoon with Doctor Babcock and Gustavus Hines. "What should I do now?" he asked, as he looked at the men, sadly.

The final opinion was that he should continue on his journey and present his problem to the Board. But how was he to go? Upon inquiry they learned that no ship bound for New York by way of the Horn would be available for several months. And since time was of the essence, Jason was discouraged. Then he learned that the *Hoa Tita* would be leaving for Mexico on February 28, which was the next day.

But there was a major problem. The *Hoa Tita* had room for only one passenger!

"Maybe the captain would allow Lucy to squeeze in with me," suggested Jason, hopefully.

"I'm sorry," replied the skipper. "There's only room for one." Frustrated, Jason paced the floor. "What, oh what am I to do?" he prayed. He watched his daughter as she played with a doll on the floor. Then he thought about Oregon. Perhaps the best way would be to remain in Hawaii and be close to Lucy. Hawaii was a needy field, and he was certain he could find employment. But as he wrestled with his problem, he was suddenly reminded of his father fighting at Lexington. In his mind he saw his father marching with the other Minute Men, saw the British commander wave his sword and heard him shout, "Lay down your arms you rebels, or else you are all dead men. Fire!" Then he saw the Minute Men prepare for action while church bells rang.

All at once Jason's eyes were moist. He remembered that Elias once said: "You're almost a spittin' image of him. You have the same blue eyes the same thick jaws, the same light hair, and the same stubbornness that possessed him. Pa never gave up!"

Yes, that was the answer! Hurrying over to the ship, he said to the captain, "I'll take that final berth."

"But what about your daughter?"

"I'll leave her in Honolulu with friends."

"As you will," shrugged the man dressed in spotless white.

With only a few hours till sailing time, Jason hurriedly made a will in which he appointed Gustavus Hines the guardian of Lucy Anna Maria Lee. He also provided funds for her education.

The next day, after a final embrace, Jason kissed Lucy goodbye and ascended the gangplank to the *Hoa Tita*.

After about five weeks of reasonably good sailing,

Jason stepped on shore at San Blas Island in Mexico. Then from Guadalajara, he headed toward Vera Cruz, which was suffering from the triple scourge of yellow fever, bubonic plague, and typhoid. He sailed to New Orleans. From there, he went by river steamship to Pittsburgh. Next he took a stagecoach and crossed the Allegheny Mountains to New York City.

The entire trip took five months.

In New York City, he found that the Missionary Board was in session; but that they were too busy discussing American slavery to consider the problems in Oregon.

Disappointed, Jason went to Washington D.C. and called on President Tyler and discussed with him the possibility of making the Northwest a United States territory. The President listened patiently. Next, Jason called on other leading men in Congress and pushed the cause of the Northwest. Having done so, he felt certain that soon the United States Congress would seize the opportunity of securing that vast and productive land.

Upon his return to New York, Jason met with the Board on July 1. As he stepped into the room and viewed the men who would decide his fate, he felt his heart thumping beneath his coat.

Soon he would learn for the first time the accusations made against him by the missionaries he had trusted and with whom he had labored.

The meeting was friendly. Doctor George Peck was chairman, and he courteously asked Jason to open the session with prayer. After prayer, feeling moderately relaxed, Jason related the history of the work. Then he answered the accusations that had been secretly hurled against him.

One criticism was that he had been irregular with his reports to the Board. To this he pled guilty. But

he excused himself by pleading that both he and
Doctor Abernathy, the bookkeeper, had been
swamped with more chores than they could efficiently
manage and that it was difficult to keep mail flowing
due to the long distances involved.

Another serious accusation was that he had engaged
in speculation. To this he answered: ''I am charged
with speculating in cattle. $250 worth fell into my
hands, they feed upon the prairies, and eat the grass
which otherwise would be burnt in the fall. I have also
purchased some eight or ten horses. I knew the
Mission must have cattle from time to time, and I will
state that my cattle were with the Mission's for a time,
but I have spent no more time with the cattle than
I should have been obliged to spend if mine had
belonged to another man.''

As humid days wearied by, and delegates kept
fanning in spite of opened windows, the numerous
accusations became exceedingly trivial. Jason had to
force himself to keep from smiling.

One accusation was that he had spent too much
time away from the mission. To this, he answered:
''As to time spent off my Mission work, I assure the
Board that the two weeks spent in attendance on these
debates at the General Conference is far more than
all the time spent for myself since my return to
Oregon.''

That reply produced some you-are-right smiles.

In answer to another accusation on speculation, he
replied: ''I made one speculation myself; I went to
Dr. Richmond's in 1842. He had some things he could
not sell. I took about $150 or $200 worth. It was a
year and a half before they reached me. He teased
me to buy his rifle for $30. At length, I consented to
take it, and on reaching home had $50 offered for it,
and let the person have it at once. That was the only

thing of the kind I ever did, and I was heartily sick of it, and am sorry I ever did it; but not because I thought there was anything wrong in it. But I was sorry I made use of it."

"There is another problem," snapped a short, fat man. Thumbs beneath his wide suspenders, he spoke like a prosecuting attorney summing up before a jury. "We sent you to Oregon to reach the Flatheads. Instead, you located in western Oregon on the Willamette. But we let that go. Now we've learned that since you moved to Chemeketa, the number of Indians you are reaching has diminished. I've also been told that you're more interested in starting a school for whites than for the Indians. Explain that."

"Indians move," replied Jason, "and many have moved from Chemeketa. But they'll return. This provides an opportunity. Didn't the Romans say: 'Seize the day'? We have seized the day, and we are now reaching many whites who eventually will be reaching more Indians than we could reach on our own."

Eventually, the questioners ran out of questions and a vote was taken. Jason Lee was found innocent on all counts. If Lee's statement had been presented to them previous to George Gray's appointment, it is improbable that he would have been dismissed.

Although they had done him great injustice, the Board decreed that he could retain his title: Missionary to Oregon.

Heartsick over the way he'd been treated, and the way the Northwest could suffer as a result, Jason decided to return to Stanstead for a much needed rest. At the time, no one realized that his dismissal would make the name Jason Lee a legend.

16

Sun Gone Down at Noon

As his stagecoach bumped and swayed over the ruts on the way to Stanstead, Jason felt disgraced, letdown, disillusioned. Instead of returning to his relatives victorious, he was sneaking home like a dog with its tail between its legs.

While passing a herd of cattle, he remembered how Jeff London had pled with him not to waste his life in the Northwest. Over a plate of buffalo hump ribs, that redhead who'd fought with the British when they burned the White House had warned: "You'll have to keep your eyes peeled for grizzly bears, scalping Indians and other hardships." But he hadn't even mentioned the perils of false brethren. And now he was a victim of false brethren!

Sick at heart, Jason's mind somersaulted back to the revival at Stanstead when Richard Pope threw out his double-dare. His challenge to surrender everything to Christ had whacked him in his middle like the knuckles of a prizefighter. But, although he had staggered, he tried to follow the preacher's advice.

While in Bible school, riding circuit, and starting the mission in Oregon, he had leaned heavily on Romans 8:28. Paul's assurance: "And we know that all things work together for good to them that love God, to them who are the called according to his purpose," had sustained him when the messengers delivered the letter which informed him that both his wife and son were dead and buried. And that same assurance had kept his shoulders straight when Lucy passed away. But now every promise on which he had staked his life seemed as useless as one of the hundreds of whitening buffalo skulls he had passed on the plains.

For a terrible moment he felt like an explorer caught in the horse latitudes and rationed to a single thimble of water each day. Indeed, he felt even worse; for it seemed that all of his sails were in shreds.

As he visited relatives, he tried to be cheerful. But try as he would, his shoulders continued to droop. He felt as if all his final examination papers had been returned with a huge F-triple minus scrawled in hideous red crayon the full length of each page.

His prayers seemed to bounce back as soon as they were uttered. He lost weight. And, even worse, it seemed that there was nothing he could do about it.

Jason, however, had not been fully discarded. Wherever he preached he faced large and enthusiastic audiences. And for a time he began to feel more optimistic. He even considered going on a speaking tour in order to raise money for the Oregon Institute which he had helped found two years before. But later in the summer he began to lose his strength. In the fall he reported to his nephew: "I have been under the doctor's care, and suffered much from the application of several large blisters, and have been so low that I could scarcely walk across the room. To do nothing, when I have apparently so much to do requires much grace; but blessed be God, His grace is always sufficient."

Late in February, Jason began to fail. Realizing he may not live long, he talked often about his beloved daughter Lucy and despaired of ever seeing her again. At least he might see Daniel once more. He dictated a letter to him and said "Turn your horse this way if you want to see me alive."

As Jason continued to sink, he remembered the poem Anna Maria had written to accept his marriage proposal. Now, he found himself mumbling:

> That hour shall find me by thy side
> And where thy grave is mine shall be;
> Death can but for a time divide
> My firm and faithful heart from thee.

In addition to the other disappointments, it was now evident that he could not even be buried next to Anna, Lucy, and his son. It was a bitter blow. He felt like a discarded rag.

While winter snows whitened the land, Jason struggled for life. As he continued to sink, he lost his power of speech. Still, his mind remained alert; and it was obvious that he recognized those who came to visit. By watching his face, it seemed to them that he was reliving the past. Some could almost visualize him standing by Lucy's grave, speaking to Peo-peo-mox-mox, viewing Multnomah Falls, and paddling up the Willamette.

Jason Lee passed away on March 12, 1845, in his forty-first year. His funeral was on the 14th. Burial was in the Stanstead cemetery. The sermon was based on Job 19:25—"I know that my redeemer liveth."

As the mourners drifted away, Daniel was heard to remark: "His sun had gone down at noon."

To many, especially non-believers, it seemed that the final curtain in Jason's life had been dropped, that he would soon be forgotten. And this belief was underlined by a pitiful event that took place about six months after his death.

When Jason handed his hurriedly scribbled will to Gustavus Hines and his wife, they took seriously the job of being Lucy's guardians. Hoping to surprise Jason, they sailed for New York City by way of China and the Cape of Good Hope, bringing Lucy with them. But when they arrived, they were dismayed to learn that Jason had been dead for six months.

Jeff London said, "Jason Lee wasted his life. He should have remained in Canada and gotten rich."

Some believers, however, were more cautious. "God often writes straight with crooked lines," maintained an elderly lady who had prayed for Jason across the years.

Since Jason was dead, Hines did the next best thing. He continued to care for Lucy as if she were his own daughter; and when he and his family returned to Oregon by way of the Oregon Trail in 1853, they took her with them. There, he moved into a home at Old Chemeketa. Since the Oregon Institute was nearby, Lucy had an excellent school to attend.

It was obvious that God still had his hand on the work of Jason Lee.

Jason had spent nearly eleven years planting seed in Oregon; and at the time of his death that seed had germinated and had just begun to squeeze through the soil. Indeed, the Oregon Trail became one of the best known routes in America. Dangerous though it was, thousands pulled their wagons through its ruts, tried to avoid the scalping knives of Indians, swam the rivers, inched over mountains, slept beneath the stars—and kept moving, moving, moving toward the setting sun.

17

The Birth of Oregon

Three years after Jason Lee's death, Sheriff Joe Meek was sent to Washington to twist the stuffed-shirts there into the Oregon way of thinking: The Northwest should become a territory of the United States.

After months of travel by foot and ship and finally by train, Joe stepped into Washington. "Where do you want to go?" asked a cabby, wincing at his passenger's worn clothes, unkempt whiskers and matted hair.

"The Coleman," barked Joe, referring to one of the most expensive hotels in the city. There, he attended a dinner for senators and attracted more attention than all of them together.

From the senator's dinner he went to the White House. At the door he noticed a doorman was a friend with whom he had played when he was a boy. Smiling broadly, he said: "Show me to the office of the President's private secretary."

"Yes, suh," responded the astonished man, flashing his magnificent teeth.

Pacing impatiently in the secretary's office, he finally said in a loud voice, "Tell the President that I'm Joe Meek from Oregon and I need to see him on important business."

The secretary jumped up and grabbed Meek with both hands. "Uncle Joe!" he exclaimed.

Within minutes, Joe Meek was sitting across from President Polk, to whom he also was distantly related. He delivered his message from the Oregon Legislature that a recent massacre of missionary Marcus Whitman and others in his settlement had made it urgent that Oregonians have better government protection. They needed territorial status.

The President directed one of his aides to take Joe to his barber, to get him a new outfit of clothes, and to show him to a room at the White House. Joe lived at the White House while Congress debated once again the controversial Oregon bill. Jason Lee had prepared the way with many of the congressmen, but Southern states were opposed to the bill because of Oregon's law forbidding slavery.

Shaved and dressed in city clothes, Joe became a sensation with the ladies. One asked him, "Are you married?"

"Yes," answered Joe, "and I have children."

"Dear me. Isn't your wife afraid of the Indians?"

"Virginia *is* an Indian," Joe replied.

The Oregon Territorial Bill at last came to a vote and passed. In the same session Joe Meek was confirmed "Marshal of the United States for the District of Oregon." Joe startled everyone by letting out a Blackfoot war whoop.

Sixty-one years after Jason Lee's death, his remains

were transported from Stanstead to Salem, now the capital of the State of Oregon, and they were buried next to those of his wives and his son. Two former governors were among the pallbearers.

One letter which was read at the memorial services related this story: "In the summer of 1860, I and my party were mercifully preserved from the wreck of a sailboat on the Columbia River, about twenty miles east of The Dalles. After hours of toil and danger we reached the north bank, wet and worn, and entered the lodge of an Indian. He was feeble in health, and impressively venerable in appearance. Our misfortune seemed to arouse all his energies.

"Being told that I was Superintendent of Indian affairs, he said he had heard of me, and was glad to see me. He then—we spoke in jargon—said we both had one God; and that he talked with that God every day. 'Who told you about the great God?' I asked.

" 'The priest,' was his reply, and immediately hurrying to the corner of the lodge he drew out a carefully folded robe from beneath a number of other packages. Within this was a dressed deer skin, then that of a badger, and a piece of bright blue cloth enclosing a small book.

"Holding it up he exclaimed: 'This is God's book! The priest gave it to me.' On opening the book, I was surprised to find it one of the early publications of the American Sunday School Union. I asked him the name of the priest. His prompt reply was 'Jason Lee.' Many years before, he told me, he had heard Jason talk first to the Indians and then to God—that is, I suppose, preach and pray—and that he had talked to that God ever since."

During President Lincoln's administration each state was invited "to provide and furnish Statues in marble or bronze, not exceeding two in each State, of deceased persons who have been citizens thereof and therefore illustrious for their historic renown, or for distinguished civil or military service such as each state may deem worthy of this National Commemoration." These statues were to stand in the National Statuary Hall of the Capitol Building.

Who should Oregon choose to honor with these statues? The answer was simple: Doctor John McLoughlin and Jason Lee.

In 1947, sculptors were selected and money provided to pay for these statues, and then a new idea gripped the state. Why not make replicas of the statues for Oregonians to enjoy at home? Citizens eagerly accepted this idea. So today, larger-than-life bronze statues of both Doctor John McLoughlin and Jason Lee stand in the Capitol Statuary Hall in Washington, D.C., and on the lawn of Oregon's own Capitol Building in Salem.

On the Capitol lawn, also, is a large bronze statue of a Methodist circuit rider on his horse. It reminds viewers that the Book of Heaven did, indeed, come to this far end of the Oregon Trail.

CHRONOLOGY

1835   Methodist Mission is established on the
       Willamette.

1836   Marcus Whitman establishes Presbyterian
       mission near Walla Walla.

1837   Jason Lee marries Anna Maria Pittman.

1838   Anna Maria and her newborn son die.

1839   Jason Lee marries Lucy Thompson.

1841   Methodist Mission moved to Chemeketa.

1842   Jason Lee helps found Oregon Institute,
       later called Willamette University.

1842   Jason's daughter, Lucy Anna Maria, is
       born and his wife Lucy dies.

1843   Oregon's Provincial Government
       established at Champoeg.

1844   Joe Meek is converted.

1844   Jason Lee is dismissed by his missionary
       board.

1845   Jason Lee dies on March 12, 1845.

1847   Marcus Whitman is killed by Indians.

1848   Oregon becomes a United States territory.

1859   The State of Oregon is admitted to the
       Union.

1906   Jason Lee's remains are moved from
       Stanstead and reburied in Salem.

1947   Bronze statues of Jason Lee and John
       McLoughlin are placed in Washington's
       Statuary Hall of Fame. Later, copies
       are erected on the lawn of Oregon's
       Capitol in Salem.

BIBLIOGRAPHY

Allen, Opal Sweazea, *Narcissa Whitman, An Historical Biography* (Binford & Morris, 1959).

Atwood, Rev. A., *The Conquerors* (Jennings and Graham, 1907).

Bancroft, H.H., *History of Oregon*, Vol. 29, 30 (Arno Press. Originally published 1888).

Bergerson, Paul H., *The Presidency of James Polk* (University of Kansas, 1987).

Bingham, Edwin, *Oregon* (Gibbs M. Smith, 1985).

Brosnan, Cornelius J., *Jason Lee, Prophet of the New Oregon* (Macmillan, 1931).

Catlin, George, *North American Indians,* Vol. 2 (Ross and Haines, 1965).

Cox, Ross, *The Columbia River* (University of Oklahoma, 1955).

Creigh, Dorothy Weyer, *Nebraska* (W.W. Norton, 1977).

Dalzell, Robert F. Jr., *Daniel Webster and the Trial of Nationalism* (Houghton Mifflin, 1973).

Drury, Clifford, M., *Marcus and Narcissa Whitman* Vol. 1, 2 (Arthur Clark, 1973).

Drury, Merrill, *Henry Harmon Spalding* (Caxton, 1936).

Fogsdale, Albert Brooks, *Royal Family of the Columbia: Dr. John McLoughlin* (Binford & Mort, 1984).

Fuller, George W., *A History of the Pacific Northwest* (Knopf, 1931).

Gilbert, Bill, *The Trailblazers* (Time-Life Books, 1973).

Irving, Washington, *Astoria, Edited by Edgeley W. Todd* (University of Oklahoma, 1964).

John, Robert C., *John McLoughlin: Patriarch of the Northwest* (Metropolitan Press, 1935).

Loewenberg, Robert J., *Equality On the Oregon Frontier* (University of Washington, 1976).

McElroy, Robert M., *The Winning of the Far West* (Putnam, 1914).

McReynolds, Edwin C., *Missouri, A History of the Crossroads State* (University of Oklahoma 1962).

Narshall, William I., *Acquisition of Oregon* Vol. 1 (Lowman and Hanford, 1911).

Nevins, Allan, *Polk: The Diary of a President* (Longmans Green, 1929).

Robertson, Frank C., *Fort Hall, Gateway to Oregon* (Hastings House, 1969).

Vestal, Stanley, *Joe Meek* (Caxton, 1952).

Whitman, Narcissa, *The Letters of Narcissa Whitman* (Ye Galleon Press, 1986).

Wyeth, Nathaniel J., *The Journals of* (Ye Galleon Press, 1969).

INDEX